FEDERAL

DEPARTMENTALIZATION

FEDERAL DEPARTMENTALIZATION

A Critique of Theories of Organization

By

SCHUYLER C. WALLACE

PROFESSOR OF GOVERNMENT IN
COLUMBIA UNIVERSITY

GREENWOOD PRESS, PUBLISHERS
WESTPORT, CONNECTICUT

The Library of Congress has catalogued this publication as follows:

Library of Congress Cataloging in Publication Data

Wallace, Schuyler Crawford, 1898–
   Federal departmentalization.

   1. United States—Executive departments. 2. United
States—Politics and government. 3. Administrative
law. I. Title.
JK421.W34 1972   353'.04   79-152615
ISBN 0-8371-6050-2

Library of Congress Catalogue Card Number 79-152615

ISBN 0-8371-6050-2

Printed in the United States of America

To

Charles Austin Beard

PREFACE

SINCE 1936, THE LITERATURE UPON THE SUBJECT OF PUBLIC administration has been tremendously enriched not merely by the reports of the President's Committee on Administrative Management, the Select Committee to Investigate the Executive Agencies of the Government, and the American Bar Association, but also by a large number of scholarly articles and monographs which have stemmed therefrom. For the most part these reports and the discussions thereof have been concerned with particular proposals for administrative reform; nevertheless, underlying many of the discussions has been the assumption that the author was in possession of the ultimate truth or else that he had arrived at his conclusions by some irrefutable scientific procedure. In certain quarters at least, it has been boldly asserted that a science of public administration is not merely a possibility but is something immediately attainable.

The most impressive thing about this discussion has been not the diversity of views expressed, but rather the fact that many of the differences of opinion were quite obviously based upon a diversity of fundamental attitudes relative to the nature of man and the character of society of which their authors were only dimly aware or totally unconscious and which at no time were brought out into the open. Apparently, even in sophisticated circles, there is no vivid recognition of the intimacy which inevitably exists between the fundamental postulates, presuppositions, and hypotheses assumed and the conclusions logically deducible therefrom.

Although the pages which follow are largely concerned

with the multiplicity of factors which must be considered and weighed in the development of the departmental structure of the Federal government, major emphasis has been placed upon an evaluation of the so-called principles of administration as applied to this particular problem from the point of view of ascertaining the degree of precision inherent in them, the extent of their interrelation with the process of government as a whole, and the nature of the fundamental assumptions upon which they rest.

Needless to say, the author does not deny the possibility of ultimately approximating a science of administration to a much greater degree than has been possible down to date. Vast segments of the field have already been reduced to quantitative measurement and still other areas will undoubtedly be brought within the range of mathematical exactitude. Significant advances in the development of a science can only be made, however, upon the basis of *all* known relevancies, and the induction and deduction of so-called laws, axioms, and statements of principle. The fact, therefore, that many of those who deal with the subject of administration are not only neglecting the interrelations between their specialty and the process of government as a whole, but are also operating upon completely unverified and in many cases unverifiable assumptions, is a matter of no slight importance. For only after the interrelationships between the conduct of administration and the operations of government as a whole have been discovered and explored, will an all-round consideration of the subject be possible. And only after a clear realization of the character of the fundamental postulates, presuppositions, and hypotheses upon which they are operating, will it be possible for either the practitioners or students of administration to recognize the nature of the intellectual operations they are conducting. Without such recognition, an accurate formulation of so-called laws or principles of administration is highly improbable. If the pages which follow contribute in any way to an increased awareness of these hitherto neglected relevancies, the author will feel fully recompensed for the time expended in the preparation of this volume.

It is impossible to thank by name the members of the administration who directly or indirectly assisted in this analysis. I should, however, like to express my appreciation to the members of the President's Committee on Administrative Management for the opportunity they afforded me to collect the material upon which this volume is based. My indebtedness to Luther Gulick's "Notes on the Theory of Organization" (*Papers on the Science of Administration,* edited by L. Gulick and L. Urwick) and to F. F. Blachly's and M. E. Oatman's *Federal Regulatory Action and Control* will be apparent to all who read these pages. I desire also to thank Professor Robert Connery for the many suggestions he made relative to the problem of departmentalization during the period of our association in Washington, and to acknowledge my indebtedness to Professor Arthur W. Macmahon for a careful and critical reading of the manuscript. Above all I wish to express my deepest gratitude to Charles A. Beard—to whom this volume is affectionately dedicated—not merely for his inestimable assistance and encouragement in connection with the completion of these pages, but also for continued intellectual stimulus over years of association with him as student, colleague, and friend.

Schuyler C. Wallace

New Milford, Connecticut
January, 1941

CONTENTS

FEDERAL
DEPARTMENTALIZATION

I ◆ ◆

THE GREAT LEVIATHAN AND
THE SCIENCE OF ADMINISTRATION

THE PROCESS BY WHICH THE GREAT LEVIATHAN HAS COME
into being and has operated in parts of the world from
time to time is a part of the history of the rise and growth
of the State. In the beginning were the acts of power by
which commanders, chieftains, and soldiers established
their dominion over large territories and subject populations.
These acts of power were followed by the creation of agencies to administer taxation, finance, police, justice, and military affairs—the guarantees of State existence. Through
the centuries, as the functions of the State increased and
exfoliated, new agencies, more or less affiliated with the old,
were established. This was true of ancient Rome from
which medieval and modern times borrowed many institutions, ideas of government, and conceptions of administrative justice. Indeed, the history of many current administrative institutions leads us far back through Anglo-Norman
times into the ages of Roman rule, especially in Gaul.

After the Roman Empire crumbled, the Christian Church,
as a hierarchy of power, survived and in some respects supplanted the Roman government, and still exists in its pris-
tine forms—a chief executive, a college of staff advisers,
archbishops, bishops, traveling agents, parish priests, and
congregations of the faithful. Concerned with the management of property, finances, revenues, and privileges, as
well as the care of souls, it has survived the revolutions of

the centuries and furnished a continuing example of administrative organization and method.

Besides the heritage of Roman institutions, both secular and ecclesiastic, has been the heritage of administrative organization and procedure connected with military affairs —one of the first and frequently the paramount interest of the State. After the rather loosely knit feudal array of the early Middle Ages was supplanted gradually by the small standing army of professional soldiers and officers of the seventeenth and eighteenth centuries, the organization and direction of armies became perhaps the first care of the modern State. For the scattered and more or less independent feudal bands, furnishing most or all of their own supplies, was substituted the single army, with its hierarchy of relationships and power running down from the commander-in-chief through the various gradations of officers to the lowest private in the ranks. In turn the army had now to be supplied by the State with food, clothing and implements of war—and this added an enormous burden to the agencies of military administration. It may be said indeed that the army was the first modern administrative system as effectively organized as the administration of the Roman Empire at its height, and that some of the greatest talent produced by Western civilization was dedicated to its improvement.

By the time the standing army had been supplanted generally by the army of universal service and even increased efforts had been made to perfect this still more gigantic aggregation of power, officers, materials, and operations, another revolution significant for administration was taking place. That was the introduction of steam and machinery on a large scale into industry, the massing of great numbers of men and women in factories and mines, and the rise of financial and industrial corporations. Out of this revolution arose on a scale never before seen in the economic sphere the division of labor, the growth of management as a specialization, and the administrative problem of organizing and directing human beings and materials. Just as Church officials shaped and managed the ecclesiastical hierarchy, as army officials shaped and directed armies, just as the State continued and enlarged its functions, now new forms of administrative organization and procedure appeared on a world-wide range, involving finances, the management of millions of people for specific ends, and the purchase, use, and sale of materials.

By the close of the nineteenth century, when administration as such was beginning to receive the attention its importance deserved, both practitioners and theoreticians had before them an immense body of concrete administrative manifestations, both historical and contemporaneous.

The growth of the leviathan of administration did not cease with the opening years of the twentieth century. If the wars of the nineteenth century were fought with mass armies greater than any the world had previously seen, those of the twentieth were to be fought by nations in arms. If the earlier phases of the industrial revolution had given rise to vast industrial aggregations, the economic integration of the twentieth century was to bring together financial, industrial, and commercial empires which in power and importance frequently rivaled the State itself. But it is in the realm of government that the growth of the great leviathan is most startlingly revealed. The laissez-faire police state is today definitely a thing of the past. In its place stand the social service, regulatory, managerial, capitalism-sustaining democracies of the West, the totalitarian states of middle Europe, and the great socialistic-communistic dictatorship of Russia.

So varied has been the great leviathan of administration in form, size, function and purpose, and so diverse have been its types from time and place to time and place, that anything like a complete classification—the beginning of science—is almost unthinkable.

At one end in the United States may be placed the simple agrarian state, based on freehold agriculture and self-sustaining homesteads with its governor, attorney general, treasurer, auditor, engineer and surveyor, and militia under elected officers. At the other, stands the federal administration of 1940 with its million or more employees, its numerous departments, boards, commissions and offices, engaged in the discharge of functions varying from the regulation of railways to the protection of public health and the distribution of social security benefits. No more fascinating story than the rise of the American leviathan is to be found in the annals of American history. But complex as the American government may seem in contrast to the halcyon days of yore, it is simple indeed when compared to the immense State bureaucracies of Germany and Russia which ramify into every nook and corner of economic and cultural life and exercise powers which can only be characterized as absolute or despotic. In Russia the direction of all branches of economy is now in the hands of the bureaucracy and practically all citizens are directly or indirectly employees of the State.

About the only generalization that may safely be made is that with the expansion of machinery, industry, transportation and communication, and with the disappearance of self-sufficing agriculture and handicrafts, the functions of government have increased, and administrative bureaucracies have swollen in size and in power.

No less bewildering than the form and size which has characterized the great leviathan at diverse times and places has been the equal diversity in spirit or purpose that these various State administrative systems have revealed.

The agrarian state in America had in effect no bureaucracy. The chief officers were popularly elected for short terms and the practice of rotation in office was a guarantee against permanency of tenure and aggrandizement of power; while even the minor employees, under the spoils regime, were, for the most part, in and out of service with the fortunes of politics. As such, state administration was not an end in itself but merely designed to serve the simple needs of a simple democratic community. The purpose of "the governing class," if Mosca's phrase is at all appropriate, was not merely to maintain itself in power at any price, but to perform temporarily certain duties deemed essential to the good order and welfare of the community and prescribed by popular representation. On the other hand, many bureaucracies in Europe have obviously been direct appendages of political power, associated with, if not drawn entirely from, a ruling class in the strict sense of the term. In such situations, the underlying purpose of the bureaucracy, like that of the ruling class, has been not only to maintain a State more or less independent of the people, but primarily to keep itself in office and power, enlarging its numbers to take care of younger sons, extending its jurisdictions, and enlarging its emoluments at public expense. It is true that some despots have called themselves benevolent and servants of the people, but in practical operation such characterizations seldom rise above euphemisms.

If, however, diversity has characterized the size, form, function, and purpose of the great leviathan, in quality, efficiency, and honesty it has likewise varied so widely as almost to defy accurate description. As one type, we may take the British administrative class in the eighteenth century, so accurately and wittily described by L. B. Namier in *The Structure of Politics at the Accession of George III.* Then and there administration was a huge aggregation of jobs, jobbing, sinecures, pensions, parliamentary politics, and public plunder. Perhaps nothing more disorganized and corrupt has ever been found under the guise of public administration, unless it was the bureaucracy of the Tsarist regime in Russia which collapsed so ignominiously in 1917. It was entirely appropriate that Namier prefaced his treatise on British government with the famous quotation from Aeschylus on birds of prey: "I took pains to determine the flight of crooked-taloned birds, marking which were of the right by nature, and which of the left, and what were their ways of living, each after his kind, and the enmities and affections that were between them, and how they consorted together."

By way of contrast, the administrative machine of Hohenzollern Germany was striking for its efficiency, ordinary honesty, and attention to economy. It was in a peculiar sense an academic bureaucracy in that its members in the upper ranges at least were drawn largely from students trained in the universities and technical schools which were themselves State institutions. Salaries were relatively low, prestige was high, promotion assured to average competence, and pensions provided for old age. Owing to the peculiar parliamentary government then prevailing in Germany, members of the bureaucracy were generally excluded from partisan politics of the more radical sort. To say that there was no jobbery in the higher branches would be to falsify history, but the rank and file of the bureaucrats seldom, if ever, shared in its pleasures and private rewards. It is doubtless correct to say that the caste system, the limitation of parliamentary powers largely to criticism, and the limited opportunities of private economy contributed as much to the efficiency and honesty of the old German administration as did the scheme

of organization, accounting, and control which characterized
the structure and operation of the administrative system. It
was German *Kultur* as well as, if not more than, rationalization that accounted for the integrity of the Hohenzollern bureaucracy.

However constituted, the role of the administrative leviathan in the fortunes of the respective countries presents both
obvious and subtle dissimilarities.

The saying that a well-organized bureaucracy is the best
guarantee against a dissolution of society undoubtedly con-
tains a large amount of truth; but the guarantee is a limited
one. Certainly a bureaucratic network, spread over a
country, and carrying on essential functions with considerable efficiency contributes to the stability of any society. Yet
the records of the past reveal that it cannot always be
counted upon in an emergency and it offers no positive assurance against calamity or even dissolution.

On some occasions, in time of crisis or revolution, the administrative bureaucracy has deserted the prevailing government. A large part of the civil and military officials of the
United States went over to the Southern Confederacy on the
outbreak of the Civil War. Such was also true of both officers
and men in the recently terminated civil war in Spain. The
Russian bureaucracy, it was alleged by the Bolsheviks,
sought to "sabotage" the Soviet Republic after the revolution of October, 1917, and the desertion of the higher and
lower ranks of officialdom, so it is asserted, accounted for
no small portion of the disorder that ensued. On the other
hand, the German bureaucracy, when confronted by a
revolution in 1918, remained in place and even if with no
little distaste served the Weimar Republic while in some
measure longing and hoping for a return to the monarchy.
Confronted with Hitlerism, it made terms with the dictator

and served his regime as it had the Republic, although many members, more or less covertly, doubtless thought they could control him in many respects and bend his will to their purposes.

To extend this consideration of the administrative leviathan to the fullness of relevant fact would be to rewrite the history of more than two thousand years, but enough has been said here to indicate both the range and importance of the subject in itself and in its relation to society and to the economic order. Whether, as some assert, the crux of modern government is administration, it is certainly one of the central problems of the modern era. The point seems to be so evident as to be beyond argument. At all events, it is so widely recognized by practitioners and students in the field of government and politics, in the largest sense of the term, that it has been made the subject of searching examination by public agencies and private investigations and so occupies a central place in all thought about the State and the determination of policies. Whether in war or peace, in ages called normal or in ages called revolutionary, the State in some form remains, and administration becomes necessary to its existence and to the discharge of the functions and powers which it assumes.

After the facts of administration came studies of administration and a search for more effective means of accomplishing particular administrative ends. This is no place to review the huge body of literature, ancient, medieval and modern, dealing with ecclesiastical, civil, military, and economic administration, nor to pay tribute to the individual thinkers of distinction, such as Comte de Guibert, whose *Essai général de tactique,* published in 1770, signaled a revolution in military administration by closely relating army organization and effectiveness with the social or national context in which military power operates. It might be deemed a work of supererogation to trace here the rise and growth of the efficiency movement in industrial administration, beginning with Charles Babbage, author of *On the Economy of Machinery and Manufactures* (1832), and coming down through the writings of Frederick Winslow Taylor and the latest pronouncements of this world-wide school of thought. It might also be regarded as somewhat antiquarian even to sketch in broad outlines the origins and development of specialization in public administration in Europe and the United States—a specialization which has produced a veritable library of books and articles on the subject and numerous official and private investigations of administrative machinery and procedures. Yet, as every science depends for its strength upon breadth, scope, range of knowledge, acquaintance with relevancies, and awareness of the historical and social context, it is appropriate for those who treat of the great leviathan to remember vividly that the whole body of practice and theory open to their examination, as guidance and check, is not contained by the contemporary scene or described in books fresh from the morning's press.

Especially is it pertinent to informed thinking about American administration to take into the reckoning the original work and conceptions of the first institution founded in the United States for the purpose of dealing with public administration in a systematic and scientific manner, namely, the Bureau of Municipal Research, incorporated in 1907. It is true that broad and objective thinking about administration in America did not originate with the Bureau, nor was it at any time confined to the precincts of that institution; but it is a matter of historical record that the Bureau was long the most active center for the study of public administration on the basis of direct observation and comparative documentation. It is true also that the first general

survey of federal administration and the comprehensive plan
for reorganization that followed therefrom were largely inspired by leaders in the Bureau of Municipal Research and
supervised by Frederick H. Cleveland, one of the directors
of the Bureau, as chairman of President Taft's Commission
on Economy and Efficiency. Furthermore, no small part of
the initial movement for administrative reorganization and
planning, municipal, state and federal, is to be ascribed to
the activities and publications of the Bureau.

Hence it is both fitting and proper in connection with any
consideration of contemporary practice and theory of administration to take into account the range of observation,
the methods and the conceptions both general and specific,
which marked the work of these pioneers in the field. What
were the assumptions or presuppositions which they took
for granted as appropriate to public administration in the
United States? How did they look upon administration, that
is, in what context of government and society? Upon what
sources of information did they draw? What were their
main axioms, maxims, or principles drawn from practice and
theory and set forth as necessary to a comprehensive consideration of the subject and as applicable in the construction or improvement of any particular system of administration?

At the outset, these early pioneers in the study of administration assumed the existence of a democratic society, popular government through a representative assembly and
elected officials and the perdurance of the conception that
the purpose of administration is to serve the requirements of
such a society with the utmost efficiency and economy. This
was, of course, a large assumption, but it was justified by
the history and practice of the United States. It was not
only a hypothesis but a more or less accurate description of
the avowed purpose of American government and the pre-

vailing practice of the country. As a starting point and controlling formula for the consideration of every phase of administration, this assumption was the basis of every discussion, proposal, and creation. It permeated all of these, underlay them, formed a persistent and inexorable part of them. This was then the governmental context in which took shape all the systematic constructions, designs, and axioms of the pioneers in the field. No aspects of administration were ever treated as something existing in a vacuum. All were related to one another and to the whole structure and process of government in American society. That was the fundamental attack on the problem more than thirty years ago, and the approach remains fundamentally sound.[1] Every system of public administration forms a part of a social organization, and its structure and procedure bear and must bear intimate relations to the spirit, form, and purposes of the government to which it belongs.

Upon what sources of information did these pioneers draw for data of administration and the construction of systematic conceptions? They used, of course, the treatises handed down by history, but they resorted especially to direct observation of administrative officers at work, including within the compass of their observations all other agencies of government in any way connected with legal authorization of administrative action, the provision of funds, and the business of scrutiny or control. Widening their range of observation beyond ordinary civil administration, these early investigators made special studies of private corporations—their structure, instruments of internal control, personnel and supply methods, standards and specifications—in other

---

[1] For supporting evidence, see Municipal Research, Numbers 60 to 80, especially No. 61, *"Constitution and Government of the State of New York—an Appraisal"*; No. 70, *"Budget Legislation in two States"*; and No. 80, *"The Elements of State Budget Making."*

words, the forms and procedures of industrial management. Collaterally, attention was given to military administration, particularly to the staff as a planning, advisory, aiding, research, and reporting agency in war and peace. In fine, they drew upon the whole range of administrative experience and theory, excepting only the ecclesiastical, and took into account, in their quest for a body of principles, all civil administration, important aspects of military administration, and the field of industrial management—each within its immediate and its more remote context.

Although the Bureau never brought together in a single treatise all elements of public administration as it conceived them, these elements were clearly explicit or implicit in its early literature. It started with and never lost sight of the whole process of government, of which administration in a narrow sense is an agency. Whether it dealt particularly with administrative organization, personnel, purchasing, budget making, or over-all management, it kept the legislature, its organization, its procedures and its politics constantly in view.

Accepting as a fundamental postulate the desirability of representative government, these early investigators at all times insisted that an efficient and responsible system of administration could be constructed and operated only if the legislative organization and procedure were adapted to adding legislative understanding and control to the supervision of the chief executive. Very early they insisted that the basic concept of industrial management, namely planning, be placed at the center of thought and practice in government; they treated the budget with its comprehensive work program as an instrument and expression of planning, and sought to make the issues presented by diversity of opinion over the work program central issues for legislative debate and political campaigns.

A survey of the early publications of the Bureau of Municipal Research reveals a concentration of attention on seven essential elements in administration: (1) a budget office in the executive department and the budget as a planned work program expressed in terms of revenues and expenditures, including costs; (2) an integrated administrative system, departmentalized and coördinated, reflected in the budget structure, and along with finances subject to legislative scrutiny; (3) personnel administration, serving all divisions of administration; (4) a central purchasing system responsible for standards and specifications throughout the administration; (5) an organization and procedure in the legislature for handling the budget as a work program expressing the policies of the government in respect of all functions assumed or to be assumed by it; (6) the adaptation of the staff system as a planning and advisory agency to serve the budget office, the head of the administration, and the legislature; (7) a scheme of accounts and controls to record for the executive and the legislature, in statistical terms, the transactions of the government and provide means of supervision and auditing.

Although the publications of the Bureau were devoted to each of these essentials, they laid repeated emphasis on the whole and reiterated warnings against the idea that sound determinations relative to any part could be made without reference to the other parts or to the underlying purposes of the entire structure.

Curiously enough, despite the widespread acceptance of the two fundamental postulates of these early analysts, first that the process of public administration can only be realistically studied in its political and social context, and second that the part is inseparable from the whole, two increasing tendencies have manifested themselves in recent years. The first of these is intense specialization; the second, deduction from abstract generalization.

Immense labors have been devoted to budgets and accounts, administrative organization in its minute details, personnel, purchasing and over-all supervision. The result has been a welcome increase in the minutiae of knowledge respecting these phases of administration and the development of a large body of information relative to the details of administrative procedure. But in this specialization, as students have gone further and further into the ramifications of each division, the reciprocal interactions of the parts and the whole have been more or less neglected, especially as regards the legislature and politics in the highest sense of that term. At the same time, comparative studies of administration, often with little reference to the social context, have produced or led to broad generalizations in the field of administration, which, in turn, have been employed as premises for deductions applicable to concrete situations. In many respects this development has contributed to the advancement of the science of administration. But specialization and abstract generalization have now reached such a stage that emphasis upon the whole setting in which administration operates and upon the concrete as against the abstract becomes once more necessary to that balanced conception of the subject which corresponds more closely to the realities of the situation.

Although this volume is directed mainly to administration —and to one particular aspect of administration, to wit, the problem of departmentalization—it is designed to raise, if not to answer, many questions which have been neglected or given only cursory consideration by writers on the science of administration. Among the larger questions, the following may be specifically mentioned. Upon what assumptions respecting the nature of society and the general processes

of history does contemporary administrative science rest?
To what extent are the axioms, maxims, rules and generalizations of administrative science of such exact quantitative or
precise descriptive character as to command that consensus
of agreement in the world of competence which permits the
laying down of imperative prescriptions? How far do differences in the purposes and objectives of various branches
of administration allow universality to any particular axioms
of administration? How far, if at all, may or should ends
other than immediate operating machinery—ends such as
liberty of person and property—enter into the determination
of administrative organization and procedure, thus invalidat-
ing more or less the axioms of an isolated science; that is,
are the same axioms valid for communist Russia, fascist
Italy, old Prussian Germany and the United States? To
what extent may or should large or ulterior purposes and
policies enter into any particular administrative organization and procedure and thus alter the applicability of
axioms devised from the immediate and apparent objectives
of that administration? When an administrative bureaucracy
has been established in particular circumstances and for
particular ends does it not or may it not tend to become an
interest or end in itself, thus to some extent limiting, if not
defeating, its original purposes? How far may or should the
conflicts of interest in society be reflected in the administrative organization and procedure which administrative science
seeks to standardize, unify and regularize, thereby hamper-
ing the strict application of administrative axioms?

These and similar questions, raised or implied in the
following pages, are not treated seriatim, nor are they suggested in disparagement of the excellent work already done.
They result from an effort to increase, rather than diminish,
the exactitude of administrative science, by including relevancies often left out of account in a quest for the utmost

simplicity. What and how much exactitude do we have in this science? In the areas where exactitude does not seem admissible by the facts of the case, what other circumstances and considerations are exigent if not imperative? Every science advances, not by devising formulas too simple for the pertinent facts, but by discovering, as far as may be humanly possible, the extent and limitations of so-called laws, axioms, or statements of principles.

II ♦ ♦

THE EXIGENCY OF
COÖRDINATION AND DECENTRALIZATION

IF THE OPERATING EFFICIENCY AND PERPETUITY OF modern government depends in a large measure upon administration, the organization and procedure of administration rest upon the twin necessities of coördination and decentralization. Here the broad axiom that coördination and decentralization are characteristics of administration is derived from the observation of actual administration and from the study of the historical processes of government in which these features appear.

The necessity for coördination is so obvious it scarcely needs documentation. If the work of a given administrative unit is to progress in a smooth and orderly fashion, it is self-evident that the activities of those participating in the enterprise must be dovetailed together. No less imperative is it, however, that under normal circumstances the work itself be subdivided and the lower ranges of supervision decentralized.

Although the mere participation of a number of individuals in a given project in itself makes necessary some division of labor, the integration of activities, up to a certain point at least, may be lodged in the hands of a single administrator. The exact point at which individual supervision breaks down varies from situation to situation. Generally speaking, the larger and more complicated the task, the greater will be the necessity for supervisory decentralization. Thus, it would be patently absurd for the head of a great university to supervise in detail the research of the various professors on his staff. The diversity of subject matter involved, ranging from entomology to epistemology, from thermodynamics to business cycles, presents a multiplicity of problems far beyond the comprehension of a single individual. To accomplish the larger purposes of the university such supervision must be decentralized. To this end an administrative hierarchy of deans, directors, and heads of departments, each with a limited degree of supervisory authority, is usually established. Similarly, it would be out of the question for the President of the United States, personally, to undertake to direct the work of the million or more employees of the federal government, much less those of the states, municipalities, counties, and *ad hoc* subdivisions as well. The truth of the matter is that no man can bring within the range of his knowledge the congeries of special problems which enter into the administration of a modern state, however great may be his mastery of general principles.

Thus, paradoxically enough, the *sine qua non* of efficient coöperation and control is the effective decentralization of supervisory authority.

Fortunately for the process of administration, two major forms of governmental organization, developed over the centuries, radically decentralize the task of administrative supervision. These forms have been established, needless to say, primarily as the result of certain political forces operating over large territorial areas and are designed to serve *political* rather than administrative ends. Inevitably, however, they have exerted an enormous influence upon the process of administration.

The first form results from the practice of decentralizing the governmental organization of the various states throughout the world in an ever descending hierarchy of geographic units—states, counties, municipalities, *ad hoc* subdivisions, etc. The degree of political and governmental authority conferred upon these various local governments differs from country to country. This variation has been due in part to the influence of geography, in part to language, in part to the measure of military security, in part to political tradition, and in part to a number of subsidiary influences too numerous to list here.

For example: the fact that the colonization of the territory now embraced in the United States occurred at a moment in the world's history when the difficulties of oceanic transportation and communication made the maintenance of centralized supervision difficult if not impossible certainly contributed to the decentralized character of American colonial institutions—a characteristic which was accentuated and perpetuated at a later date in our political development by the equally great difficulties inherent in the centralized government of a continental domain. In similar fashion, the broad expanse of territory encompassed both by the British Commonwealth of Nations and by the United States of Brazil has likewise exerted a decentralizing influence upon their respective political institutions.

The truth of the matter is that, in all three countries, the tremendous diversity of geographic conditions in these vast territories has made both legislative and administrative uniformity undesirable, if not impossible. And it has given rise to a demand for both political and administrative autonomy.

Of less importance than the sheer size of the territories embraced, yet not without significance, has been the influence of river valleys and mountain ranges. Thus the physical configuration of its Alpine terrain has effected the political organization of the Swiss Republic.

Also noteworthy in determining the development of political institutions has been the diversity of nationality and language within a number of countries in central Europe. The fact that certain of the Swiss cantons are German not only in their language but in their ethnological derivation, that others are French, and still another, Italian, has in and of itself been conducive to the maintenance of a federal rather than a unitary form of government in the Helvetian Republic. Diversity of nationality and language was also largely responsible for a degree of decentralization of the old Austro-Hungarian Empire. And it is, even today, one of the most powerful centrifugal forces in Europe.

A third significant factor in the evolution of political forms has been the relative degree of military security attained by the various nations of the world at different stages in their development. The high degree of military security which has, until recently, been the heritage of the English-speaking people has without question contributed heavily to a decentralization of political institutions rarely found elsewhere.[1] On the continent of Europe, the ability to mobilize the entire military resources of a nation at a moment's notice has often been the paramount necessity. Political and administrative centralization rather than decentralization has consequently been the institutional virtue most highly prized. This has been as true of democratic France as of both pre-Nazi and Nazi Germany. As a result of this and other forces, with a few striking exceptions, the major countries of the Continent have inclined to a centralized rather than a decentralized form of government.

[1] The Swiss Republic, the Austro-Hungarian Empire, and the old Kingdom of Poland constitute three outstanding exceptions to this generalization. In the first two, the centrifugal demands of nationality and language triumphed over military necessity. The fate of the Kingdom of Poland still stands, however, as a solemn warning of the price which may be paid for extreme geographic decentralization in the face of military insecurity.

Even under these circumstances, however, the difficulties both of uniform legislation and centralized administration have given rise to more or less provincial and municipal autonomy. To this, the provincial and local governments of France, Germany and Italy all stand witness. So advantageous is governmental decentralization both politically and administratively, that the use of this pattern of organization in some degree is well-nigh universal.

A fourth factor which has, at times, exercised a decisive influence in determining the extent to which the governmental organizations of the various nations of the world have been decentralized geographically is the political tradition peculiar to each. To some extent these political traditions have been the result of the very forces we have been discussing. Once crystallized, however, they have exerted an influence of their own. Thus, although the conditions which gave rise to the Jeffersonian concept of democracy in the United States have long since passed away, this concept has continued to exert a powerful influence upon the course of public policy, lending support to the states'-rights tradition and accentuating the demand for municipal home rule. Similarly, the political traditions which have evolved both in the British Empire and in the Swiss Republic have constituted a significant force in the maintenance of the decentralized character of their respective institutions. By contrast it should be noted, also, that the Napoleonic tradition of France and the militaristic tradition of Prussia have each exerted an influence in the contrary direction, contributing to the integration not merely of the military aspects of these governments but also to the centralization of their civilian functions as well.

It is impossible within the confines of a single chapter even to discuss the subsidiary forces which in this country and in others have contributed further to decentralization.

In some countries the relative competence of the national as against the local bureaucracies has played a part; in others, the rise of economic problems which could only be solved upon a national scale; in still others, the sheer accident of personality seems to have been crucial at times.

For the most part, as already indicated, the determining factors in the development of local institutions have been political and economic. They have, nevertheless, exerted an enormous influence upon both the organization and the processes of administration. In some respects this influence has been highly advantageous in the orderly conduct of government; in others, distinctly detrimental.

In so far as the geographic decentralization of political institutions has resulted in allocating to the subordinate units of government various functions which can be administered independently of the central government, it has undoubtedly lightened the administrative burden where otherwise it would be heaviest, i. e., upon the central administrative hierarchy and its chief executive. And in doing so, it has, in the democracies at least, transferred a portion of the ultimate supervision of the local administration to that segment of the electorate most vitally concerned with the administrative problems within its jurisdiction. It has done so, moreover, without any serious, complicating disadvantages.

To the degree that the decentralization of political institutions has resulted in delegating to various subdivisions administrative functions which are inextricably intertwined with the activities of other units of government, it has undoubtedly complicated the process of administration. Even in these circumstances, of course, the advantages of decentralization, both politically and administratively, may more than offset its defects. Nevertheless, the growing interrelations of modern economic life, and in consequence, of governmental activity, have increasingly accentuated the fact that, although the decentralization of political organization along geographic lines offers the advantage of administrative devolution, it is usually lacking in adequate machinery of administrative coördination.

The merits and defects of this form of governmental organization, both politically and administratively, are strikingly illustrated by recent developments in the United States. By virtue of the constitutional provision that "the powers not delegated to the United States by the Constitution, nor prohibited by it to the States, are reserved to the States respectively or to the people," distinct spheres of governmental activity were seemingly allocated to the federal and state governments respectively. In consequence each state administered its own educational system with little or no regard for the federal government or for the other states; each state conducted its own financial operations, subject only to the constitutional provisions regarding such matters as the emission of bills of credit and taxation; each state enforced its own criminal laws as the exigencies of local politics demanded. In other words, the relationship between these various units of government was purely federal in character, i.e., each unit had a sphere of activity in which it was supreme, in which it operated subject to little or no control save that imposed by its own electorate.

Similarly, except for such limited and sporadic supervision as the state legislatures might from time to time exercise, American municipalities and other units of local government were allotted spheres of authority within which they might carry on functions of government delegated to them without reference either to the activities of adjacent communities or of the states themselves. With the rise of state administrative supervision over cities, this situation is, in many particulars, a thing of the past. Nevertheless, even today, municipalities usually administer street-cleaning services, fire departments, building departments, etc., in whatever fashion local interest or sentiment decrees. In so far as these strictly municipal affairs are concerned, the relation of the local unit of government to the state government continues to be essentially federal.

Coöperation between these various units of government has not been impossible. Far from it. In certain fields at least a considerable measure of coördination has been worked out. This is evidenced not only by the accomplishments of the Commissioners on Uniform Laws, the Council of State Governments, and the innumerable conferences of state administrative officials, but also by the fact that the streets and highways of one community usually dovetail into those of the next, that local fire departments generally come to the aid of an adjacent community faced with a conflagration beyond its control, that local police departments are both willing and anxious to apprehend criminals sought by neighboring communities or by far distant states.

In so far as those units which are legally independent of each other are concerned, however, this coöperation and coördination of activities has been entirely voluntary—the result of a process of negotiation.

In connection with those matters upon which there is well-nigh universal agreement both as to the proper objective of government and as to the procedures to be followed in attaining the desired end, intercommunity agreements have been relatively easy to consummate. Indeed, under certain circumstances, no formal agreement has been necessary. The police of a neighboring community or adjacent state are, as has already been intimated, just as eager to arrest a criminal who has violated the generally accepted criminal code as are the police of the community in which the crime has been committed. The maintenance of law and order and the protection of property are universally accepted objectives of government.

In those situations, consequently, in which no coördination between these various governmental units is necessary, or in which such coöperation as may be necessary will be forthcoming spontaneously, it is apparent that this geographic decentralization of political institutions is entirely satisfactory from the administrative point of view. Under these conditions the absence of a mechanism of administrative coördination is, of course, no serious inconvenience.

But the number of situations in which the spontaneous coöperation of the various units of government can be depended upon is limited. This is true even in connection with the enforcement of the criminal law. During the slavery era, for example, the police in certain of the Northern states were neither anxious nor willing to coöperate in the enforcement of the fugitive slave law. And even today, in connection with those extraordinary situations in which, according to the mores of a sister state, the punishment does not fit the crime, refusals to acquiesce in requests for extradition are not unknown. The situation is even more aggravated when the possibility of integration is complicated by a maze of technical detail. Thus the mere task of working out the technical problems involved in the proper coördination of the police forces of adjacent communities is usually sufficient to prevent the attainment of such a coördination.

Examples of the failure of attempts at intergovernmental coöperation might be multiplied indefinitely. The fact is that coördination by negotiation is frequently a slow, cumbersome and at times an impossible process. Hence whenever the administrative activities of the various units of government are in fact intermeshed, whatever may be the political merits of the situation, the administrative defects of this mode of organization may much more than offset its administrative advantages. Whether such is the case in any particular instance can only be determined in the light of the circumstances surrounding it.

It is interesting to note, however, that the very same forces which are giving rise to administrative difficulties in connection with the geographic decentralization of governmental institutions are similarly complicating its operation politically. For example, during the last several decades we have seen emerge in the United States a series of problems seemingly incapable of solution on a state or local scale. This has been particularly true in the fields of agriculture, large-scale industry, labor, and relief. Conceivably certain of these problems might have been worked out through the medium of interstate and regional compacts. But so cumbersome and complicated would have been the process, so difficult would have been the task of integrating one set of state statutes with another that no serious proposal embodying the idea was ever put forward. Instead, the federal government has taken the leadership in the attempt to cope with these problems, and in the process has so transformed the relationship of the states and localities to the federal government that many commentators are inclined to characterize the new fabric of government as national rather than federal. Although the bulk of the field work is still being carried on by the states and the localities, the ultimate power of supervision and direction has, in many cases, been transferred to Washington. As a result the older, more extreme form of political decentralization which has characterized the United States, historically, is breaking down. An increasing political and administrative burden is being carried on by the central government.

This tendency is all the more significant not merely because it is world-wide, but also because it is occurring at a period in the world's history when governments are embarking upon vast public enterprises and stricter regulation of private undertakings.

It is becoming increasingly obvious, consequently, that some technique other than the traditional devolution of political power upon a geographic basis must be perfected to make possible an adequate decentralization of supervisory activities, and at the same time to permit a degree of administrative coördination impossible with the political geographic decentralization of the past. Only thus will it be feasible to keep the great administrative leviathan under control and assure a high degree of efficiency in its operation.

A second mode of political organization which has, historically at least, diffused the burden of administration and contributed to the decentralization of supervisory authority in the various geographic units which we have been discussing, is the practice of decentralizing the machinery of administration along functional lines. For want of a better phrase, it might be called functional devolution. This form of organization was most widespread in the United States during the Jacksonian era. Indeed, it might be said to have been the dominant administrative characteristic of state government during this period. Although in a number of states the governor was theoretically charged with responsibility for the entire state administration, supervisory powers commensurate with his responsibility were rarely, if ever, granted. Not only, as a rule, did he lack the power to appoint or remove the heads of the administrative units which were theoretically subject to his control, but usually he had the power neither to require reports, to inspect, nor to issue orders. Instead, independently elected lieutenant governors, attorneys general, treasurers, engineers, superintendents of education, and other officers headed what were in fact separate units of administration. Such supervisory power as was exercised was wielded by the electorate through the medium of the ballot box or by the legislature through appropriation bills or organic acts.

This extreme segmentation of the administration, resulting as it did from the direct election of the chief administrative officers of the state, has in a considerable measure passed away. Its influence, nevertheless, still lingers. Although most of the states no longer elect ten or twelve administrative officials, the practice of electing various state officials is still common.

In many jurisdictions, moreover, the practice of gubernatorial or legislative appointment of administrative officers for long and frequently overlapping terms of office has perpetuated this devolutionary concept in actual practice. Thus, state boards of education—or regents—are frequently appointed in a way intended to protect the school administration from gubernatorial dominance. Such, also, very often is the case with boards of health, departments of labor, tax commissions, utility commissions, and the other so-called quasi-legislative, quasi-judicial agencies.

For the most part, county governments are still organized on a disintegrated basis. Independently elected sheriffs, coroners, and tax assessors each continue to head various segments of the county administration.

A somewhat distinct variation of the practice has been introduced into those commission-governed cities in which the charter allocates particular departments or bureaus to certain specified commissioners. In the absence of any centralizing authority, the inevitable result appears to be the disintegration of municipal administration into three, five, or seven independent administrative establishments, as the case may be. This development, it should be noted, however, was contrary to, rather than in accordance with, the expectations of the proponents of the plan.

Until comparatively recent times, administrative segmentation or devolution has not been an outstanding characteristic of the federal administration. Such administrative devolution as has existed has been largely hierarchical in character and has usually followed departmental lines. With the creation of the Civil Service Commission in 1883 and the Interstate Commerce Commission in 1887, however, the segmentation of the federal administration began. From that day to this, an ever increasing number of so-called quasi-legislative, quasi-judicial agencies has been established, each more or less independent in its own peculiar sphere.

The reasoning which has inspired this method of organization has varied from situation to situation and from decade to decade. The extreme functional decentralization which characterized the Jacksonian era was designed not so much to reduce the burden of administration at any particular center as it was to render the administration sensitive to popular control, and incidentally to reduce the concentration of power in the hands of any single individual. Its motivation, in other words, was largely political. Similarly, the creation of a series of independent boards and commissions was designed primarily to protect these agencies from political pressure. The movement for the commission form of municipal government received its impetus from the relative efficiency of the emergency government established in Galveston, Texas, after the tidal wave of 1900. At the time of its adoption, the commission plan was thought to represent a concentration rather than a decentralization of political power. It was assumed that the small board would handle all important matters as a group. Only after several years' experience was the fact revealed that this mode of governmental organization contained within itself the seeds of its own disintegration.

Whatever the reason, an incidental consequence of the organization of units of government in this fashion has been the decentralization of the administrative burden which would otherwise have fallen upon the chief executives of these diverse geographic units and their principal administrative subordinates. Whether the use of this method of political organization has accomplished the purposes for which it was intended is exceedingly dubious.

At the moment, the general consensus of opinion holds erroneous the old Jacksonian concept that the frequent election of numerous administrative officials is necessary to the maintenance of democracy. Similarly, the belief that the commission form of city government automatically produced a superior municipal administration has largely been abandoned. The extent to which the newly created independent agencies have justified the reasoning underlying their establishment is a matter of dispute.

One thing is obvious. Inherent in this form of organization is the same administrative difficulty we have been discussing—the lack of an adequate mechanism of administrative coördination.

Here, too, however, a considerable degree of coöperation can be achieved through the voluntary efforts of the occupants of the different offices, particularly in those matters concerning which there is general agreement as to the proper objective of government. This is natural, for as Luther Gulick has pointed out, "in an old stable community small enough for each person to know the other . . . the town board, the school board, the park commission, the overseer of the poor, though answerable to no single executive, manage to get along with each other, and each to fit his part of the work into that of the others to arrive at a sensible

result for the whole picture . . . Even the competing busi-
nesses generally work along together in harmony."[2]

Under certain conditions the degree of coördination which
may thus be attained is quite adequate for the normal operations of government; under others, the political advantages which are presumed to be inherent in this pattern of
organization are thought more than to offset any administrative disadvantages to which it may give rise. This in general
is the line of reasoning advanced by the schoolmen in defense of an independent educational system. It is also frequently adduced in behalf of the quasi-legislative, quasi-
judicial commissions.

In many situations, however, it is quite obvious that such
a chain of reasoning is the purest sophistry—that in fact
this method of organization is both inefficient and un-
economical. For just as the increasing complexity and in-
terrelatedness of modern life has reduced the usefulness of
extreme geographic decentralization, so have these same
forces—to an even greater extent—been undermining the
utility of the functionally segmented organization. The fact
that the degree of interrelation between the administrative
units of a given governmental area either is, or appears to be,
much greater than that which exists between the governmental functions of separate geographic entities inevitably
contributes to the criticism and abandonment of this segmentation. In the final analysis, most of the administrative
agencies in a given governmental area draw their financial
support from a common body politic. In consequence, maladministration in one particular affects not merely the administrative unit directly concerned but all other services.
Moreover, the lack of coöperation between the various administrative agencies in the same geographic area becomes

[2] *Papers on the Science of Administration*, edited by Luther Gulick
and Lyndall Urwick (New York, 1937), p. 38.

more obvious and seemingly less excusable than lack of coöperation among autonomous geographical districts.

A result of the forces thus generated has been the gradual abandonment of the administrative segmentation which so frequently characterized the central government for a hundred years in a number of states, and a continuous pressure for its discontinuance elsewhere. A tendency toward integration rather than disintegration marks the newer state constitutions. Similarly, the more highly integrated city-manager form of organization has replaced the commission form as the dominant trend in municipal government. And although the creation of independent boards and commissions has characterized both state and federal governments during the last several decades, it has been more and more subjected to attack, despite the fact that in recent years the members of many of these commissions have been made subject to appointment and removal by the Chief Executive—a radical departure from the earlier procedure in various cities and states.

We may reasonably expect a continuance of this trend. The increasing complexity of modern life and, in consequence, of governmental activity, gives rise to a demand for a greater and greater degree of administrative coördination. The result has been, and in so far as one can see will continue to be, a radical reduction in the sphere of governmental activity in which the voluntary coöperation of the heads of independent administrative establishments will in itself be adequate to effect the necessary coördination.

Thus, at the very time governments are assuming greater and greater administrative responsibilities—in large measure perhaps because of this fact—another traditional method of political organization (which has had the incidental but nevertheless exceedingly important consequence of decentralizing the administration) has revealed such deficiencies that in some circumstances it has been completely abandoned; in others, its usefulness has been radically impaired. It is increasingly apparent, consequently, that some other mode of organization must be used to carry the burden of administration hitherto diffused along geographic and functional lines.

The third great historic method by which administrative responsibility has been decentralized is, of course, the practice of departmentalization. It would be manifestly absurd, as we have already intimated, for the chief executive of any large governmental unit to undertake to direct personally the thousands of employees subject to his supervision. Not only would it be physically impossible for him to amass the factual background upon which each of the day-to-day and hour-to-hour orders must rest; but it would be equally impossible for him to issue the orders. Effective coördination of the hour-to-hour activities of the men who are actually engaged in carrying out some particular enterprise can only be secured by someone immediately at hand. The necessity of organizing the subordinate personnel into a series of groups or work units, and the delegation of a limited degree of supervisory authority to a subordinate supervisor or foreman has been universally recognized. These work units, it may be remarked parenthetically, may be organized upon the basis of the job to be done, the process used in doing the job, the persons or things dealt with, or the place in which the service is rendered. All other things being equal, the more homogeneous the work unit, the more efficient its supervision is likely to be.

In a very small administrative unit, the organization of the personnel into a series of work units and the delegation of a limited degree of supervisory power to the foremen thereof may suffice. Such, however, would not be the case in a larger and more complex organization, for even after this initial grouping, the supervisory burden imposed upon the chief executive would still be beyond his capacity. It would be manifestly ludicrous, for example, for the commander-in-chief of an army to attempt to maintain direct communication with every corporal under his command. A further grouping of the subordinate personnel is obviously imperative. Squads must be organized into companies; companies into regiments; and regiments into army corps. Similarly in civilian administration, work units must be organized into divisions; divisions into bureaus; and bureaus into departments. And in each case greater and greater supervisory authority must be delegated to the administrative officers in charge of each unit. In this fashion alone is it possible to reduce the administrative burden upon the chief executive to such a point as to bring it under his control.

Ultimate power continues to reside in the hands of the chief executive, but the hour-to-hour, day-to-day and even week-to-week supervision of activities is delegated to subordinate officials. By virtue of the decentralization inherent in the process, an otherwise impossible problem is reduced to manageable proportions.

In contrast to the two principles of political organization previously discussed, however, the process of departmentalization, it should be noted, is not merely a technique of decentralization but a method of coördination as well. Indeed from many points of view its primary purpose is or may be coördination.

Thus the organization of the subordinate personnel into a series of work units has for its primary objective the development of a degree of coördination not otherwise attainable among the individuals assigned to a particular task. Such supervisory authority as the corporal or foreman may exercise is directed toward this same end. Similarly, the grouping of squads into companies, companies into regiments and regiments into army corps, or alternatively, work units into divisions, divisions into bureaus, and bureaus into departments has an identical objective.

The chief difference between this form of organization and those previously discussed lies in the fact that each of the units of administration is subject to the ultimate control of a single supervisory official. For the most part coöperation will still be achieved on a voluntary basis, attained either spontaneously, or through the process of negotiation. Indeed, one might almost say that the degree by which coördination is achieved on this basis in and of itself constitutes an index of the morale of the organization. Nevertheless, behind these voluntary efforts at coördination lies the power of command, affecting not merely the eventual outcome but the process of negotiation itself. Thus, although the coöperation of individual employees in a given work unit will probably be largely voluntary, the fact that the supervisor is empowered to discharge a noncoöperative or recalcitrant employee may in and of itself stimulate coöperation. Similarly, although the exact relations between two bureaus in a given department may be worked out by the process of negotiation, the mere existence of a departmental superior may conceivably expedite the negotiations. In the final analysis, the matters in dispute can be settled by executive fiat.

Thus, as can readily be seen, the process of departmentalization has a distinct advantage over the two methods of organization analyzed previously in that it not only makes possible a high degree of supervisory decentralization, but in that it also provides a method of coördination.

Needless to say, the technique of departmentalization has gained such well-nigh universal acceptance that it might justifiably be characterized as a principle of administration.

Despite the general acceptance of the principle, however, a number of important problems arise in connection with its application. Among these the more important are the following: How many departments should there be and what size should they be permitted to attain? Should they be organized upon a hierarchical or devolutionary basis? Upon what principles should the subordinate administrative units be allocated places in the departmental structure? What machinery—if any—should be established to insure inter-departmental integration? To what extent should cognizance be taken of the play of powerful political forces? What is the role of the legislature in the process of administration?

These are a few of the questions which arise in connection with any attempt to apply this principle to the organization of the administrative branch of any large-sized unit of government.

III ♦ ♦

QUANTITATIVE CONSIDERATIONS
IN DEPARTMENTALIZATION

THE UTILIZATION OF THE PRINCIPLE OF DEPARTMENTALI-
zation in the administrative branch of the government
immediately raises the problem of the number and size of
the departments to be created. This, in turn, raises several
subsidiary questions. Important among these is the relation
which the departmental structure should bear to the chief
executive, the influence that structure may exert both upon
the character of the departments established and upon the
quality of their management, the effect it may have upon
the chief executive's cabinet and, finally, its influence
upon administrative-legislative relations.

The essential purpose of the technique of departmentalization is, as we have already indicated, the diffusion of
supervisory authority in such a way as to relieve the chief
executive of an otherwise intolerable administrative burden,
and the creation of a mechanism of coördination adequate
to the exigencies of administration.[1]

One of the primary considerations in the development
of a departmental structure involves the number of administrative subordinates a chief executive is capable of
handling, for "just as the hands of man can span but a

[1] In connection with this and the two succeeding chapters, the author
wishes to acknowledge his indebtedness to Luther Gulick whose
"Notes on the Theory of Organization" (*Papers on the Science of*

limited number of notes on the piano, so the mind and will of man can span but a limited number of managerial contacts." [2] If then the heads of the administrative departments of a given governmental unit are to maintain direct contact with the chief executive, the number of administrative departments established must be kept within his span of control; but in fact a warning is necessary: the word "span" is a metaphor, not a measurable reach, and the number of interviews a chief may have with his subordinates in a day depends in part upon their special abilities and the nature of the problems presented for decision.

This axiom of limited span is, of course, no new discovery but is indeed the fundamental postulate upon which the concept and practice of departmentalization rest.

Despite a universal acceptance of this principle, no consensus exists as to its specific application. Upon the basis of his military experience, Ian Hamilton concludes that three administrative subordinates is the maximum number with whom a chief executive should come into immediate contact. As a result of their researches Major Urwick and V. A. Graicunus set the maximum at five or six. Viscount Haldane and Graham Wallas, on the other hand, believe that a chief executive can supervise as many as ten or twelve without undue burden.[3] Diversity rather than unanimity characterizes opinion on the subject.

It is interesting to note in this connection that in 1937 the chief executive in Japan appeared to be in contact with the heads of some thirteen administrative departments; in Canada, Germany, and Italy, fourteen; in France, seventeen; in Russia, nineteen or twenty; and in England, twenty-

Administration, edited by L. Gulick and L. Urwick, New York, 1937) to no small degree stimulated the writing of this volume.

[2] *Papers on the Science of Administration*, p. 7.

[3] *Ibid.*, p. 8.

six.[4] The situation in Washington was in many respects peculiar. Nevertheless, it is not without significance that the President of the United States, for a number of years, has been supposed to coördinate the activities of some sixty administrative subordinates.

To what extent the development of this diverse departmental structure represents a variety of concepts of the chief executive's span of control, and to what extent it has been the result of other forces is, of course, impossible to determine. Nevertheless, the mere fact that administration has nowhere broken down is itself significant. Although there is undoubtedly some connection between the number of administrative establishments immediately subordinate to a chief executive and the effectiveness of his supervision, the inefficiency which may result from the imposition of a burden upon him beyond his capacity is manifestly one of degree rather than of a character immediately catastrophic in its consequences. It is, of course, conceivable that the inefficiencies thus engendered may, over a period of time, pile up so many administrative difficulties that some future crisis which might otherwise have been surmounted may prove catastrophic.

It is difficult, moreover, to ascertain with anything approximating scientific precision the exact boundaries of a chief executive's span of control. That such must be the case is easily explicable. In the first place, tremendous individual diversity in administrative capacity characterizes the chief executives who have in times past presided over the major administrative units of the world. Thus the speed with which

---

[4] It may well be that the number of direct managerial contacts maintained by the chief executives of these various nations is somewhat larger than appears on the surface. If such is the case, it adds force to, rather than detracts from, the arguments contained in the ensuing pages.

Mussolini assimilates information in contrast to his ministerial associates is a matter of widespread comment in Rome.
The extent to which Sir Robert Peel was conversant with all
departmental questions in contrast both to his predecessors
and successors in office has elicited comment from English
constitutional historians. In the second place, great diversity
in capacity is also found among the secretariats with which
chief executives have been surrounded. Incapacity in subordinates has loaded otherwise able men with divers degrees of
inconsequential detail, or, equally important, it has furnished
them with memoranda of decidedly uneven quality, upon
the basis of which action must be taken. In the third place,
the difficulties of administration vary from situation to
situation. For example, the head of a post office or a department of public works, in which the work is similar in
character, can more easily maintain effective supervisory
contact over a large number of subordinates than can the
head of an army, with elements as diverse as infantry,
ordnance, aviation, communications, chemistry, transport,
and engineering, each of them presenting a separate set of
problems, all of them awaiting his ultmate decision in general
or precise form. Similarly, the number of individual contacts which can be maintained in an old, stable organization
where the work has been largely routinized, where new problems are few, and interviews between the chief executive
and his subordinates infrequent, can easily be larger than
in a new or dynamic organization where changing circumstances necessitate much more frequent consultation between the chief executive and his subordinates. Finally, the
ease with which supervisory contacts can be maintained
where the organization is all housed in a single building or
even located in a single city is much greater than it is if
the administrative organization involved is scattered from
Washington to San Francisco, from London to Calcutta.

The conclusion to which these facts lead is that the boundaries of a chief executive's span of control cannot be easily ascertained and described in a mathematical formula of universal application. Instead, they must be discovered through the study of each specific situation, and will be largely determined by a number of impressions, by a combination of relevant knowledge and practical judgments, rather than by any scheme of scientific measurement.

This is not equivalent to saying that the measure or concept of the chief executive's span of control can exert no influence upon the development of the departmental structure. Far from it. In certain situations, such as that which existed in Washington in 1938, there was a consensus of opinion both among students of public administration and among practical administrators that the administrative organization was out of control, that no chief executive, however able, could possibly coördinate effectively the activities of more than sixty independent administrative establishments.

But whether the number of direct managerial contacts with the chief executive should be reduced to three, as Ian Hamilton insists; to ten or twelve, as Viscount Haldane and Graham Wallas believed, or to twenty or twenty-five, as Russian and British practice respectively suggests, is in fact a controversial question.

In this connection it is pertinent to note that whereas in those countries in which the subordinate administrative units have been grouped in a few large departments there has been little or no criticism of the departmental structure; in each of the countries which have experimented with a multiplicity of small departments or other administrative establishments, the volume of criticism which has arisen in connection with the administration thereof has from time to time assumed serious proportions. Moreover, this criticism has come from the practical administrators rather than from the mere theoreticians. In Great Britain the administrative crises caused by the first World War not only brought about a temporary reorganization of the British executive and the creation of a supercabinet in an effort to achieve a coördination of departmental activities not otherwise attainable, but it was indirectly responsible for the formulation of Lord Haldane's famous *Report on the Machinery of Government* in connection with which he suggested a reduction of the existing number of administrative departments in Great Britain to ten or twelve. The attempt of ex-Premier Blum to superimpose six ministers of coördination upon the existing departmental structure of France similarly constitutes a striking testimonial to the unsatisfactory character of the French experiments with a multiplicity of departments.[5] Although experts attached to the President's Committee on Administrative Management and the Select Committee to Investigate the Executive Agencies of the Government disagreed on a number of points, there was no disagreement among them on the necessity of a radical reduction in the number of purely administrative establishments directly subordinate to the President.

In any event, the criticism which has arisen in each of the countries in which a multiplicity of departments or independent establishments has characterized the administrative structure is itself noteworthy, the more so by virtue of the fact that in many cases it emanates from the very men who have been administering the government. Their testimony is, as we have already indicated, rendered the more impressive by the relative absence of criticism from

[5] In this connection, mention might be made of the growing practice in Italy of concentrating a number of departments directly under Mussolini in an effort to attain greater coördination.

administrators occupying similar positions in more highly centralized administrative organizations.

The ultimate decision as to the number of departments and the size thereof cannot be made solely upon the basis of the chief executive's proper span of control, however. Important as is the direction of the administrative structure from the top, it is only one of a number of factors. No less important is the influence that the departmental structure itself may be expected to exert both upon the character of the individual departments and the character of their management, and the effect this structure may have upon the quality of the cabinet and upon administrative-legislative relations. It behooves us, therefore, to consider the effect which the various departmental patterns now extant throughout the world have upon administrative operations at the departmental level.

Although the diversity in the number and size of the departments now existing in the major countries and their chief geographic subdivisions may suggest an equal variation of opinion as to the desirable number of administrative departments, the fundamental cleavage is between a small number of large departments and a large number of small ones. In the world of practical affairs the contrast is best illustrated by the ten great departments which until recently formed the center of the administrative organization of the United States or the thirteen which encompass the national administration in Japan and the twenty-six departments into which the British administration is divided. All departmental arrangements are certainly to some extent based on one or the other of these concepts—or are compromises between them.

The argument in behalf of large and therefore relatively few departments rests first, in the opinion of its proponents, on the degree of coördination thereby attained. By virtue

of the existence of an executive officer immediately superior
to the administrative units which constitute the department,
the line of demarcation between these subordinate units can
be more clearly delineated; overlapping activities and duplicating personnel can be minimized if not eliminated; intradepartmental disputes can be adjudicated; and a degree of
coöperation not otherwise possible can be achieved.

Thus, to make use of an illustration from American history, had the United States Public Health Service and the
Children's Bureau been in a single department, the long-
drawn-out conflict relative to the respective jurisdictions
of these two agencies would have been settled long since by
an order from the head of the department; whereas the
historic set-up permitted the controversy to drag along for
years, to be straightened out only recently through the slow
and cumbersome process of interdepartmental negotiation.
Similarly, if the United States Employment Service and
the Works Progress Administration had both been subject
to the same administrative superior, the lack of coöperation
which has from time to time marred their relationship would
in all probability have been investigated at its inception and
a *modus vivendi* agreed upon, or the issue would have been
settled by administrative order, instead of being permitted
to continue as a source of irritation to all concerned. If
the Land Office and the Division of Grazing, both of which
are now located in the Department of the Interior, had in
times past been consolidated with the agricultural units of
the Department of Agriculture in a Department of Land
Utilization, the notorious conflicts between these several
units would likewise have been avoided.

Illustrations might be multiplied indefinitely. The simple
fact is that the chief executive of a major political unit is
too immersed in other activities to pay much attention to
the coördination of relatively trivial, but in their mass

tremendously important, details of administration. Only when a given situation becomes notorious will it, under ordinary circumstances, be brought to his attention.

But, it may be asserted, this is merely an argument for sound departmentalization which would justify the creation of a multiplicity of small departments as readily as it does the development of a more limited number of large ones. True! The basic reasoning which underlies the creation of either small or large departments is the same. Both make for a degree of integration not otherwise attainable.

Wherein then lies the difference? The difference lies in the fact that, *up to a certain point* at least, the larger the department, the greater the degree of coördination possible between the subsidiary administrative units.

Just as small departments make possible the more efficient coördination of the activities of a limited number of bureaus, so a large department permits the coördination, not only of a greater number of bureaus but of units of administration as large as the small departments themselves. Although the mere existence of the Department of Labor and the Federal Security Administration makes possible the internal coördination of their respective subdivisions, the integration of these and related units into a single great Department of Social Affairs would make possible a more effective coördination of their several activities. Thus the periodically unsatisfactory relations between the Works Progress Administration and the United States Employment Service could be ironed out, and the operations of the Social Security Board and the Bureau of Labor Statistics still further consolidated. Similarly, the development of a Department of Land Utilization would make possible the integration of the activities of a large number of bureaus now scattered here, there, and elsewhere.

The line of reasoning just advanced holds good only up to

a certain point, however, for just as there are limits to the chief executive's span of control, so also are there limits to the control which can be exercised by any of his subordinates.

No less important is the fact that the advantages of departmental coördination are fully applicable only to administrative units engaged in related activities. Thus, whereas the allocation to a single administrative department—no matter how large—of the administrative agencies functioning in the fields of relief, agriculture, or transportation should eventuate in a more effective coördination of these activities, no such result could be expected to follow the integration of a similar number of units chosen at random. The assignment of the Bureau of Labor Statistics, the Pure Food and Drug Administration, the Division of Postal Savings, the Marine Corps, and the Farm Credit Administration to a single department for the sake of achieving some theoretical size would be obviously ludicrous.[6] The argument for large departments rests on the assumption that such departments will parallel broad fields of related activities.

In addition to increasing the potential effectiveness of the day-to-day and week-to-week coördination of the various subordinate administrative units, the development of large departments paralleling broad fields of human endeavor also makes possible, so the protagonists of this mode of departmental organization insist, comprehensive planning. Thus, the fact that the Department of Agriculture, with a few exceptions, encompasses within its jurisdiction the full sweep of governmental activity in the field of agriculture facilitates the development of plans involving every aspect of the field. This is illustrated not only by

[6] For a detailed discussion of the basis of departmental integration, see pp. 91 ff.

the research and educational activities of the Department
but by the soil conservation and marketing program as well.

In striking contrast stand the various governmental agencies dealing with the problem of transportation. Dedicated,
until comparatively recently, to the regulation of certain
aspects of railroad operation, the Interstate Commerce Commission was compelled by its legislative mandate to confine
its thinking and its activities largely to this form of transportation. Similarly, the Bureau of Public Roads could plan
only in terms of automobile transportation; the Civil Aeronautics Authority only in connection with airways; the Maritime Commission and the Corps of Engineers only in terms
of water transport.

The division of the field of transport among a number
of independent agencies has certainly hampered, if not
blocked entirely, the development, within the administrative
structure of the federal government, of any agency whose
function it is to work out plans for the solution of the transportation problem as a whole. Instead, such measures as
have been formulated and adopted have been fragmentary
in character, frequently affecting adversely those aspects of
the transportation system whose interests have not been fully
considered in their formulation.

The question may be raised as to whether planning should
be carried on at the departmental level at all, or whether
it should not remain the exclusive prerogative of the chief
executive, upon whose shoulders rests the constitutional responsibility of from time to time giving "to the Congress
Information on the State of the Union," and recommending
"to their consideration such Measures as he shall judge
necessary and expedient."

A moment's consideration, however, will reveal that planning must take place at all levels. And that the chief executive simply could not report on "the state of the union" un-

aided. Thus in the development of the national forests it is the technicians attached to the Forest Service, and not the chief executive, who must plan the work of the Bureau in reforestation, fire protection, and lumbering. Similarly, the initial responsibility for the development of plans for mobilization in the event of war rests with the two military departments, and not with the President. The Department of Agriculture has quite correctly assumed the initiative in working out plans for the solution of various agricultural problems. The disorder prevailing in the National Recovery Administration by contrast will long serve as an illustration of ineptitude, marking the imposition of a hastily improvised plan from the top.

The conclusion of this line of reasoning, however, is not that over-all planning centered in the chief executive is futile. Far from it! Had the National Recovery Administration been more carefully excogitated in the President's Office, the possibilities of its success might have been greater. A multitude of problems will continue to transcend departmental lines, no matter how effectively the departments are organized. And finally, there will always be a question of coördinating the proposals which emanate from the departments.

Nevertheless, both European and American experience suggest that administrative planning is usually more effective when participated in by those actively engaged in the management of the administrative units which will be called upon to carry out the plans evolved.

The only real question is whether the various agencies of the government should be dedicated independently to the administration of some limited segment of a given field, thus rendering planning for the entire field difficult if not impossible, or whether they should be integrated into departments sufficiently large as to encompass the sum total of government activities in each field, thus facilitating planning on the departmental level. Both European and American experience would seem to suggest the latter.

A collateral but nevertheless exceedingly important consequence of the increased coördination (both of day-to-day administration and of planning) made possible by the development of large departments is economy of operation, and financial saving. A still further advantage is the fact that larger departments tend to minimize the disintegrating or dominating influences of pressure groups. These groups, in times past, have often exercised a paramount influence over particular departments or independent establishments. The Veterans Administration, for example, is generally conceded to be under the influence of the American Legion. Similarly, although the Department of Labor is by no means dominated either by the A.F. of L. or the C.I.O., the influence of organized as over against unorganized labor in the operation of the department is usually decisive.

In large departments these pressures, to some degree at least, tend to cancel one another. The heads of large departments, consequently, can, if they so desire, take a broad statesmanlike view of their problems rather than a view dictated by the necessity of placating certain organized pressures. Thus, the creation of a Department of Social Affairs encompassing labor, social security, health, education, welfare, and pensions would, it is urged, be infinitely superior to the retention of the existing Department of Labor and the development of a new Department of Public Welfare. The enlarged Department, so it is maintained, would protect the management thereof both from the dominance of organized labor, and the no less insistent demands of the welfare workers. Neither the labor, nor welfare nor health nor education forces would permit the subjection of the department to the ends of any particular group. The result would be that the departmental management could take a more balanced view of the problems encompassed within its jurisdiction.[7]

As the sheer size of a department helps to generalize its interest, as the pressure groups cancel each other's influence, so it also minimizes the necessity for complicating the administrative structure with a congeries of so-called quasi-legislative, quasi-judicial agencies. (The point is elaborated later in our analysis.) Similarly, the necessity for cutting past the vested interests that have dominated the smaller departments—one of the major reasons for creating a number of the independent administrative establishments—is also reduced. The simplification of the administrative structure which should result would itself be a gain in operating efficiency.

No less important a reason for the development of large rather than small departments, as the devotees of this method of administrative integration see it, is the influence these departments may be expected to exert not only upon the quality of departmental management but also upon the entire administrative personnel.

In their opinion, the very complexities of the management of a large department should tend to compel the politically appointed heads to delegate the actual management of the department's routine to professional administrators, and to confine their own activities to the determination of the broad lines of departmental policy, the maintenance of legislative

[7] It should perhaps be conceded, however, that this is a general rather than a universal phenomenon. Thus, although measured in terms of the personnel employed, the Department of State is a small department, such is the multiplicity of pressures converging upon this single department that to a great extent they too cancel each other. It cannot correctly be said that the Department of State is subservient to any particular interest. Despite these and other exceptions, the dominant trend would appear to be the one set forth in the paragraph immediately preceding.

contacts and the task of interpreting their departments to the body politic—functions more nearly within their comprehension and grasp. The embryonic beginnings of professional management in the existing Departments of Agriculture and Treasury, both large departments, merely foreshadow, so it is asserted, a development which is inevitable as departments grow in size and complexity.[8]

It seems reasonable to assume, moreover, that the very same forces which have placed the heads of the overwhelming majority of administrative subdivisions of the existing departments upon a professional basis will continue to operate in connection with the larger departments wherever they are created. The result should be an extension of the merit system upward to include those larger groupings over and above the bureau level into which these larger departments might be divided. This development would rest not merely upon those demands for governmental efficiency which have been largely responsible for the extension of the civil service down to date, but also, as we have already indicated, upon the increased complexities of the departments themselves. Thus the administrative heads of the Labor, Social Security, Health, Education, and Welfare sections of a huge Department of Social Affairs, if such a department were created, would sooner or later, it seems certain, be drawn from the permanent service.

In the beginning, the heads of these larger groupings would in all probability be political appointees. And, in one sense, they would have a no more difficult task than that imposed upon the politically appointed heads of small departments or independent establishments at the present time. Nevertheless, the fact that the primary responsibility for the management of the whole department must rest upon

[8] For an elaboration of this point see A. W. Macmahon and J. D. Millett, *Federal Administrators* (New York, 1939), pp. 25ff.

the head of the department, would probably cause him to cut past the political appointees in the department to the men who really know, rather than to permit the information necessary for his decisions to filter through a series of politically appointed administrative amateurs. Similarly the bureau chiefs would undoubtedly continue their customary policy of appealing over the heads of the political novices who may be placed at the head of any grouping of bureaus to the secretary of the department. If this should occur, the result would be the imposition of a direct supervisory burden upon the head of each of these large departments far beyond his administrative capacity. The upshot might well be the extension of the merit system to the point where it would include not merely a professional departmental manager but also a corps of assistant managers, drawn from the permanent service, allocated to the head of the great divisions into which the bureaus would be grouped, or alternatively assigned to the supervision of such specific functions as finance, personnel, and publicity.[9]

The influence of the further professionalization of the administration which the development of large departments should stimulate would in all probability extend far beyond a mere increase in efficiency in the services thus manned. The extension of the merit system to offices far more responsible than any now open to the civil service should attract into that service many persons possessed of real administrative ability, who now shun government employment because of the limited opportunities at the top. A tuning up of the whole civil service should follow.

A still further result should be the reduction of the num-

[9] Although the problem of the internal organization of the departments is connected with the one we are discussing, it is nevertheless a distinct and separate problem. For an extended analysis of this problem, see Macmahon and Millett, *op. cit.*

ber of foci of bureaucratic imperialism now existing and the direction of the energies of ambitious bureau chiefs into channels of greater operating efficiency.

At the moment, owing to the fact that advancement beyond the bureau-chief level is largely blocked, ambitious administrators, with some notable exceptions, tend to satisfy their urges by striving to extend the scope of authority allotted to the administrative units under their respective jurisdiction. Each bureau chief so inclined rationalizes his endeavors either on the basis of the extraordinary administrative efficiency of the unit under his control, or on the ground that the additional function desired is intimately related to some activity already under his direction. In fact, however, many of these attempts at bureaucratic aggrandizement are the result of the frustration of able and ambitious men. As a consequence it seems probable that administration support is given to many projects which might otherwise be viewed with scepticism; or alternatively, many activities are assigned to particular agencies which might more effectively be administered elsewhere.

If the development we have forecast takes place, the integration of all intimately related administrative units into a single large department should, to some extent at least, exercise a restraining influence on this imperialism, for it imposes upon the small administrative units another supervisory officer who, by virtue of his experience in the permanent service, should be fully cognizant not only of proposed duplications of effort, but also of the logical place in the administrative structure to which new activities should be assigned. The extension of the merit system to more responsible administrative positions, moreover, should not only elevate the ablest and frequently the most aggressive bureaucrats into positions more nearly commensurate with their abilities, but it should result in a reorientation of the energies of those who remain in charge of the subordinate units, for presumably with such a development, "departmental-mindedness" would be a *sine qua non* of further promotion.

Whatever may be the effect of the creation of large departments upon the administrative personnel, it should certainly have a beneficial influence upon the character and, in consequence, the operation of the Cabinet. Although it is by no means axiomatic that Lilliputian departments lead to Lilliputian thinking, nevertheless there is an element of truth in the epigram. The head of a small department or administrative agency is very likely to confine his thinking to the limits of the field subject to his jurisdiction. Although such astigmatism is not universal, it is all too general. Conversely, the head of a great department encompassing within its scope the full sweep of a given field of human activity is under the stimulus of planning for the solution of problems in all aspects of the field, which should in itself be conducive to broad and statesmanlike thinking. To become specific, whereas the Interstate Commerce Commissioners, the members of the Maritime Commission, and the chiefs of the Bureau of Public Roads and the Civil Aeronautics Authority need only think about certain aspects of transport, railroads, steamships, automobiles, and airplanes, respectively, the head of a Department of Transportation would be invited if not compelled to think not only about each of these specific means of transportation but about their interrelations as well. The result should be both an improvement in the calibre of cabinet officers and in the discussions which take place at cabinet meetings.

The development of a limited number of large departments, moreover, should radically reduce the number of jurisdictional disputes between the departments which are now brought to the chief executive for adjudication. All other things being equal, the larger the departments, the greater the number of problems which can be settled at the departmental level.

The fact that these interdepartmental controversies rarely come up at cabinet meetings is only partially relevant. Considerable time is consumed by "a word with the President" both before and after cabinet meetings and at special conferences. And out of the unsettled interdepartmental controversies arise personal attitudes on the part of cabinet officers which color their attitudes on questions of public policy.

The point may be made that interdepartmental conflicts will continue to exist, no matter how large the departments may become. True. But, as has already been pointed out, the number should be greatly reduced. And no less important, the character thereof should be radically changed. Trivialities, at least, should be settled within departmental confines. The controversies which remain should, consequently, possess, in part at least, the character of differences of opinion over questions of public policy, and as such be worthy of cabinet consideration.

Proponents of the larger departments point out still another advantage: the simplification of administrative-legislative relations. More than sixty administrative agencies were in 1936 introducing measures into Congress sometimes as outgrowths of duplicating and conflicting purposes. These were allocated to Congressional committees in such a way as to make difficult if not impracticable the complete coördination of legislative measures. The result was not merely a duplication of committee hearings and committee discussions, but occasionally the enactment of somewhat inconsistent statutes.

The integration of the various administrative units into a limited number of large departments would certainly reduce the continuous duplication of requests on the part of administrative units for similar or identical authority, and should introduce a greater degree of cohesion into the general system of administration. For it can be taken for granted that the present tendency to insist upon departmental clearance for all legislative proposals which is now to be found in the more efficiently managed departments would characterize the proposed larger departments. By virtue of this development the present confusion and duplication of work imposed upon the legislature should be minimized as the number of conflicting demands are radically reduced.

If the development of large departments possesses a number of apparent advantages, it involves also a number of seeming disadvantages which merit thorough consideration.

Critics of this mode of departmentalization insist first that it necessitates the interposition of one more individual between the men who know, i.e., the heads of the small departments and independent agencies, and the chief executive who must ultimately decide. This means not only an inevitable delay in the transmission of information both to and from the chief executive, but worse than that, it means that the departmental secretary will, in all probability, be less fully cognizant of the detailed operation of his department than he would be if he were the head of a smaller unit, and in consequence less capable of presenting either an accurate or a clear-cut picture of the needs of his department.

Moreover, unless the enlarged department is well organized, or the head of the department is a man of unusual administrative ability, capable of delegating great masses of detail to administrative subordinates, he will find it exceedingly difficult if not impossible to keep abreast of the matters which pile up on his desk. The result may well be interminable delay in handing down decisions relative to departmental policy, the postponement of bureau action, and a slowing down of the whole administrative process. Complaints about the existence of bottlenecks are not unknown in the departments in Washington even as they exist today.

This situation is all the more likely to be aggravated by virtue of the fact that in the formation of large departments the illusion of the necessity for close and continuous coördination is frequently mistaken for the reality, with the consequence that the bottleneck at the secretary's desk is clogged by the unrelated character of the divers problems presented. Thus, had the proposal to allocate to a single Department of Finance the Reconstruction Finance Corporation, the Farm Credit Administration, the Home Owners Loan Corporation, the Federal Housing Administration, the Securities Exchange Commission and the other fiscal agencies of the federal government been accepted in connection with the 1938 reorganization, it would have concentrated on the secretary's desk such unrelated functions as the real-estate operations of the Home Owners Loan Corporation, the stock-market regulations of the Securities Exchange Commission, the specialized credit activities of the Farm Credit Administration, and the banking regulations of the Federal Reserve Board. The consequence might well have been confusion twice confounded. If by any chance the Secretary of Finance or Treasury should be the type of individual who finds it difficult to delegate responsibility, the log jam on his desk might shortly block the wheels of government. At best the machinery of government would be complicated unnecessarily.

No less undesirable administratively, as the critics see it, is a second illusion which the development of large departments frequently produces—the illusion of self-sufficiency. The fact is, of course, that no department, however large, can embrace within its jurisdiction all aspects of the many problems with which it will be confronted. Again and again situations will arise which will require both interdepartmental consultation and action. In connection with its soil erosion program the Department of Agriculture will time after time impinge upon the engineering activities of the Bureau of Reclamation or the Corps of Engineers. Aviation landing fields are of interest not only to the Civil Aeronautics Authority of the Department of Commerce but to the State, War, Navy, Post Office, and Treasury Departments as well. Illustrations might be multiplied indefinitely. The problems which can be handled effectively only by interdepartmental consultation and coöperation are numerous and important.

The danger is that owing to its size a large department may assume that it is capable of handling all the facets of a given situation, when such in fact is far from the case; and that, in consequence, the chief executive and even the legislature may be committed to a particular policy before all aspects have been thoroughly studied. In so far as the development of large departments is conducive to such a result, their creation may well be considered a disruptive rather than an integrating force.

The allocation of all interrelated activities to a single large department, moreover, despite what was said previously, may lead to a situation conducive to administrative or managerial sabotage. For example, there is reason to believe that if the Resettlement Administration had been launched under the aegis of the Department of Agriculture, it would have died of maladministration almost at birth. The Department of Agriculture had been historically oriented to serve the interests of the intelligent, aggressive, moderately prosperous farmers. In no sense of the word had it been a welfare agency. At the time the Resettlement Administration was conceived, the Department of Agriculture was probably no more interested in rural welfare work in behalf of the submerged fifth of the agricultural population than was the Department of Commerce in indigency in the urban area. Indeed, in so far as rural welfare work of the kind undertaken by the Resettlement Administration succeeded in raising the standard of living of the submerged groups either by making them agriculturally self-sustaining or by providing them with alternative employment, it would run counter to the immediate self-interest of the Department of Agriculture's clientele. For, in either case, it would mean a diminution of the labor supply and an increase in farm wages. Whether the architects of the Resettlement Administration were justified in their fears is a controversial question. The fact remains, the Resettlement Administration was initiated as an independent agency.

A similar line of reasoning underlay the independent status of a number of other New Deal agencies which might logically have been incorporated in one of the existing departments.

From the point of view of our discussion, the important point is not whether the sponsors of these measures were correct in their estimate of the consequences which would follow the allocation of these various administrative units to their logical places in the departmental structure. The important point is that the adoption of the principle of the integration of *all* subordinate administrative units into a limited number of large departments paralleling broad fields of human endeavor makes possible exactly that administrative or managerial sabotage which the proponents of the measures feared.

Thus, far from creating an administrative machinery which automatically makes for a greater degree of coördination and efficiency in the execution of the laws of the land, the development of large departments may in fact create a situation which makes possible their frustration.

No less important than the deleterious results which the development of large departments may have upon the process of coördination, in the opinion of the sceptics, is the influence they may exert upon the administrative personnel. Whether as able men could be persuaded to become cogs in a huge departmental organization as are now willing to take over the management of the independent administrative establishments is very dubious. Not only would the prestige now attached to the headships of these independent agencies be radically reduced by virtue of their subordination to the large departments, but, more important, the degree of freedom now enjoyed by the heads of these various establishments in working out the solution of their respective problems would be similarly affected. And, needless to say, prestige and independence are two of the great factors in inducing able administrators to enter the government service. One can only wonder whether the very efficient administrators who have at one time or another headed the Farm Credit Administration, the Federal Home Loan Bank Board, or the Reconstruction Finance Corporation, respectively, could have been persuaded to enter government employment if all of their actions had been subject to the approval or disapproval of an immediate departmental superior, to whom, incidentally, the bulk of the credit for their administration would have gone.

Despite assertions to the contrary, there is no assurance, moreover, that the creation of large departments will lead to an extension of the career systems upward. In the opinion of the opponents of this method of administrative integration, the contrary may well be the case. The very size of the department will make the problem of civilian control over the bureaucracy appear to be a more difficult one. This will undoubtedly be seized upon by advocates of democratic control and by spoilsmen as an excuse to push the system of political appointment downward rather than the merit system upward. In consequence, Congress may well insist not merely that the heads of the present independent establishments and their satellites be retained on a politically ap-pointed basis even after they have been integrated into the departmental structure, but that the heads of any of the great divisions into which the departments may thereafter be organized be similarly appointed. The result will be even more demoralizing than the situation which now exists. For, although at the present time the heads of the independent establishments are for the most part political appointees, and in consequence transitory officials, only a limited number of such appointees now stand between the technicians and the chief executive. Owing to the direct contact between the bureau chiefs and the individuals who are to place their problems before the chief executive, the "education" of these political appointees is not insuperable. If, on the other hand, an additional set of political appointees is interposed between the chief executive and the technicians, the process of "education" becomes much more complicated, and in all probability less effective. It should occasion no astonishment, therefore, if, under these conditions, an increasing number of errors were made in the transmission of information both to the head of the department and to the chief executive, with an inevitable decrease in administrative efficiency throughout the whole administrative branch of the government.

By contrast to this, the prospects for the merit system in the small departments are satisfactory indeed. Conscious of mastery of their respective administrative units, fearing no bureaucratic dictation, the heads of these smaller establishments may easily distinguish between aspects of their task which involve questions of public policy and those which are entirely administrative in character, and delegate the handling of administrative detail to the permanent service. The embryonic beginnings of this development may already be seen in the Departments of State and of Labor, both of which are small departments. The fact that this development has not proceeded further is largely due to a variety of forces—politics, inertia, etc.—which have little or nothing to do with this aspect of the departmental structure. How little the size of the departments under the present circumstances has to do with the extension either of the spoils system or the career service is indicated by the negligible concessions which have been made to the spoilsmen by the Tennessee Valley Authority in contrast to the inroads they have made in the Public Works Administration. So few have been the concessions made by the Tennessee Valley Authority that rumor has it that the administrators thereof have from time to time run into serious congressional difficulties. Rumor also reports that at one time fully forty percent of the appointees to posts under the Public Works Administration found it necessary to secure political clearance—this despite rather than because of Secretary Ickes.

It is impossible on the basis of such experience to conclude, however, that small establishments are more impregnable than large to the assaults of the spoilsmen. The peculiar circumstance surrounding each agency has created a situation so unique that generalization is dangerous. It is quite evident, however, that size is not necessarily the decisive factor.

Size does, nevertheless, play an important role in the expedition of the public business. Owing to the more limited number of decisions which must be referred to the top, it is frequently much easier for the head of a small administrative establishment to keep abreast of his work than it is for the head of a large department to do so. The bottleneck or "log jam" which so frequently characterizes the administration of large departments is relatively unknown in smaller agencies. The illusion of self-sufficiency and the possibility of managerial sabotage, to which reference has already been made, can likewise be avoided.

No less important for effective administration is the fact that the smaller departments may expeditiously retain the vitalizing influence of intimate relations with various and sundry so-called pressure groups. And that such relations may be vitalizing rather than destructive is illustrated not only by the operation of such small units as the Children's Bureau but by the functioning of numerous other divisions both of the Departments of Labor and of Agriculture.

That the effectiveness of the Children's Bureau is closely tied up with the intimacy which exists between this administrative unit and the various welfare organizations, the head of the Children's Bureau would be the first to admit. Similarly, the efforts of the Extension Service to coöperate with the Granges and other agricultural organizations, to promote the organization of 4H clubs, etc., reveal an intense desire to develop and maintain increasingly intimate relations with its agricultural clientele. In so far as the integration of the various administrative units into a series of large departments reduces the intimacy of the relationship between these units and those segments of the population which they are designed to serve, the effect may be more disadvantageous than desirable. But do not the very illustrations used indicate that a satisfactory degree of intimacy between an administrative unit and its clientele can be maintained even though the administrative agency is a subordinate unit in a departmental structure? After all, the Children's Bureau has long since been an integral unit in the Department of Labor;

the Extension Service, part and parcel of the Department of Agriculture.

The question involved is not one of black and white, but one of degree. It is significant to note consequently that in the Department of Agriculture there is incessant complaint that the mixture of promotional and regulatory functions in a single department constantly interferes with the most effective administration of both. A recent Under Secretary of the Department of Agriculture went so far as to tell the author that until the two functions had been divorced neither could be administered with the efficiency that would be otherwise attainable. The development of that degree of intimacy between the department and its clientele in connection with promotional activities which is desirable would be continuously curbed by the fear that such intimacy might seriously interfere with the administration of the regulatory functions, and vice versa.

The point can, perhaps, be made even more clearly in connection with the proposed Department of Social Affairs. Although the inclusion of the Department of Labor in a great Department of Social Affairs encompassing within its jurisdiction such matters as labor, social security, health, education, and welfare, might, as its proponents assert, be conducive to a more scientific approach to the problem of labor than takes place under the existing organization, it might also carry in its train objectionable consequences. Would the Division of Labor of such an enlarged department, for example, be as aggressive in serving the needs of labor as is a Department which was in large measure the creation of organized labor and which continues to depend on labor and its allies for political support? Might not the office of Education be prostituted to ends remote from education? In other words, would the relationship of the various units to their respective publics in such a department be as effective as it is at the present time?

Moreover, would not the so-called scientific approach to problems of public policy very shortly take on the characteristics of entrenched bureaucracy?

Also undesirable, in the opinion of a number of opponents, is the influence which the creation of a limited number of large departments would have upon the chief executive's cabinet. As has been indicated previously, the heads of relatively small departments can in a very short space of time get to know their departments inside and out. Discussion of problems consequently can be based upon an intimate first-hand knowledge of the subject under consideration. In this they stand in striking contrast to the heads of great administrative departments, who would be dependent, as are some of the department heads even today, upon one-page summaries of particular situations prepared by some administrative subordinate; or who must, alternatively, bring to each discussion a battery of experts to furnish the factual data they would otherwise lack. Thus the discussions of the heads of small departments alone can partake of the nature of reality; the discussions of the heads of large departments unaccompanied by their experts would of necessity partake of the superficiality likely to be found in a convocation of newspaper editors.

The mere multiplicity of small departments makes it possible to introduce into the cabinet representatives of more varied interests and lines of thought than is otherwise possible. And the fact that the chief executive's cabinet is frequently not merely an administrative but also an advisory agency on broad questions of public policy makes such representation highly desirable. The present Secretary of Labor, for example, concedes that her time is almost as much taken up advising the chief executive on broad questions of labor policy as it is in the administration of her own department. An independent Department of Labor and Works Progress Administration made possible the presentation of the labor point of view at Cabinet meetings and the transmission of the "welfare" point of view at those more private, but frequently more important, conferences which Harry Hopkins formerly attended. With the welfare units grouped together, their point is now more formally canalized. Quite a different situation would exist, however, if labor, social security, health, education, and welfare were all grouped in a large department, primarily responsible to the head of that department. Inevitably wherever a conflict of views existed, one point of view or another would have to be sacrificed. And in consequence, the chief executive would fail to receive whatever wisdom there may be in a multitude of counselors.

There is the possibility, of course, that a large number of departments may produce a cabinet too unwieldy for consultation. Certainly the assemblies of the National Emergency Council, to which both the heads of the various departments and the independent establishments were from time to time summoned, more nearly resembled mass meetings than discussion groups. However, it should be noted that the British with a Cabinet of some twenty and the French with a Cabinet of thirty or more both seem to utilize the cabinet organization more effectively than is the case in the United States. Incidentally, it is by no means imperative that all department heads be included in the formal Cabinet. As a matter of fact the Postmaster did not enter the Cabinet until Jackson's administration, despite the fact that the office had been functioning from the very beginning.

The net influence which an all-embracing departmental organization would have upon administrative-legislative relationships is also controversial. Large departments, it is true, might well contribute to the consolidation and coördination of the requests of subordinate administrative units for legislative action. But an even more effective consolidation and coördination, intra- and inter-departmentally, might be achieved through centralized clearance, i.e., the requirement that all administrative requests for legislation be cleared through the budget bureau or other executive agency. In this fashion the various and sundry measures emanating from the departments and agencies might be consolidated and conflicting proposals ironed out. Such a procedure would obviously eliminate in this particular any advantage the larger departments would have over smaller ones.

Just what results would flow from the so-called "neutralizing effect" which the development of large departments might have upon the play of "pressure" influences is much more difficult to forecast. Would the pressure groups, when they found it was no longer possible to persuade administrators to yield to their importunities merely accept defeat? Or would they turn their attention to Congress and write their desires into the statutes in great detail? If they should resort to the latter device the outcome would be worse for administrators. At the present time the statutes are usually sufficiently flexible to permit of "accommodations." If these "accommodations" are written into the statutes their increased rigidity may much more than offset any advantages which the "neutralization of the departments" may have.

Thus it becomes evident that there are distinct advantages and disadvantages attached to the creation either of a limited number of large departments or a greater number of smaller ones. On the one hand is the presumption that the development of a limited number of large departments will (a) reduce the number of managerial pressures upon the chief executive to a point more nearly within his span of control; (b) achieve a greater degree of coördination between the various administrative units in connection with their day-to-day activities than would otherwise be probable; (c) increase the possibility of broad-scale planning at the departmental level; (d) minimize the pernicious influence of pressure groups; (e) reduce the necessity for establishing independent agencies; (f) improve the quality of departmental management and personnel administration; (g) exercise a beneficial influence upon the quality and calibre of the cabinet and improve administrative-legislative relations.

On the other hand, the creation of such departments may well result in (a) interminable delay in executive decisions and a consequent slowing down of the whole administrative process; (b) an illusion of self-sufficiency that may lead to the neglect of many interdepartmental aspects of a given situation such as would not take place under the alternative form of departmental organization; (c) administrative or managerial sabotage; (d) an extension of the spoils system downward and a consequent deleterious effect upon personnel; (e) the loss of the vitalizing influence of administrative-clientele intimacy; (f) a deterioration of the quality of cabinet discussion; and (g) increased administrative-legislative difficulties.

On the basis of this analysis it becomes apparent that few, if any, conclusions having the validity of a formula or law in hydraulic engineering or synthetic chemistry emerge or can, in the nature of things, emerge. It is evident that quantitative measurement has slight application to this aspect of the problem of departmentalization. Undoubtedly the number of departments which a chief executive can competently supervise and assume responsibility for is limited, but the quantitatively measurable operations of administration are not such as to permit a purely quantitative determination of the limit, and thus fix definitely the degree or extent of departmentalization. No approach to the solution of the problem can be made on the assumption that all administrative operations have an identical or even similar character, or that any given act of administrative arrangement is permanent, or that a given set is the same over any large span of time. Nor can such an approach be realistically made until we have a far more minute analysis of those aspects of administration which are entirely or largely routine and hence subject to quantitative determination of some kind, and until fine distinctions are drawn between the routine and the qualitative or policy-involving operations of administration. It is the variations in these last, needless to say, which upset all attempts to work out a mathematical formula.

Despite the fact that it is customary to separate administrative from legislative operations and to treat administrative operations as if they possessed some identity of nature, little or no effort has been made to determine that identity in fact. Pending a finer analysis of this problem, we may certainly say with assurance, on the basis of the above presentation of relevancies, such disparities of operations exist from department to department that indices of identity common to the administrative operations of all departments are difficult if not impossible to discover above the level of mechanical, clerical, and other routine performances. Until such indices, if they exist, are discovered, quantitative determination of the number of departments required by the end of efficiency in supervision and operation are out of the question. Yet we can say with some certainty that the amount of routine or quantitatively measurable activity does vary from department to department, and that this has a bearing upon the problem of departmentalization.

It is evident, for example, that the relative amount of routine in the War Department in time of peace is far greater than the relative amount of routine in the Department of Agriculture or in the Interstate Commerce Commission. Indeed, the statutes governing the three agencies respectively indicate somewhat roughly the degrees or areas of routine and policy determination.

Since this is so, it follows that it is not the number and variety of administrative functions alone which should be paramount in determining the degree of departmentalization in the interest of efficiency in supervision and control. The factors of routine operation and judgment must enter into consideration. It would be easier for a chief executive to supervise and assume responsibility for twenty or thirty large departments of smooth-running routine than to assume the same obligation for four or five small departments in which crucial matters of policy, entrusted to the administrators, involve broad questions of public policy committed to the keeping of the chief executive by our political system.

The problem thus posed is complicated by the element of time and circumstances. Even a superficial knowledge of history discloses the fact that great changes are made from period to period in the emphasis on administrative functions and the arrangements for carrying them into execution. For a long time the Department of Agriculture was limited to functions mainly trivial and routine. By accretion and by reason of the agricultural crisis, it has become one of the most important departments from the point of view of the public policy with which the President of the United States is of necessity concerned. A crisis in foreign affairs or a war brings the State Department and the war agencies of government into prime consideration, without any revolutionary changes in administrative organization. Forecasts of such coming changes are difficult to make, but the high degree of probability that great changes will come to pass must enter into any realistic computations of administrative science. Conceivably, then, effective supervision might be exercised over a large number of departments at one time and in one set of circumstances, whereas such would not be the case at another time and in other circumstances. As an illustration, we need only to refer to the administrative questions confronting President Coolidge in 1928 and President Roosevelt in 1933. An effort to make a quantitative determination of the number of departments an abstract consideration divorced from time and circumstances is an operation in a vacuum. And realistic science includes all known relevancies.

Yet, greater exactitude in the matter of departmentalization is not out of the question. The range of data could be widened. Closer studies of administrative operations based on the distinction between routine (or somewhat quantitative) operations and judgment-involving can and should be made for use as a basis in determining the nature and degree of departmentalization. In this fashion a considerable advance may yet be made toward precision and exactitude in the matter. But it may confidently be expected that when mathematical measurement has reached its fullest limits, room will be left for human judgment, both empirical and expert.

IV ♦ ♦

COÖRDINATION VERSUS OPERATING
AUTONOMY IN DEPARTMENTALIZATION

THE OLDEST AND MOST PERSISTENT FUNCTION OF GOVERN-
ment is war and preparation for war. All early branches of
civil administration, such as police, justice, and finance,
were organized under the direction of kings as war lords.
The first armies of war bands, though loosely organized, had
leaders and associate leaders accompanied by crowds of
followers. As the loose feudal array was supplanted by the
standing army and as the standing army was supplemented
by the army of universal service, the hierarchical principle
of organization was applied with increasing strictness to all
branches of the military services.

Accompanying this historical development was the creation of a permanent bureaucracy of officers and the founding of military schools for the study of war and the training of officers. In time the study of military administration
produced whole libraries of books and large bodies of doctrine which were widely employed in Europe and in the
United States in war offices and institutions for military
training. Inevitably nationalized military organization and
procedure exerted a profound influence on every phase of
administration, both in the development of civil departments
of government and the organization of business and other
forms of private enterprise.

Until recently the basic principle of military organization has been hierarchy—the decentralization of decreasing

degrees of supervisory authority to ever descending levels, together with the retention of final authority at the top. Thus, although the commander-in-chief of a modern army may delegate supervisory power to the generals, brigadier-generals, colonels, lieutenant-colonels, majors, captains, lieutenants, sergeants, and corporals under his command in ever descending order, the ultimate authority continues to reside at the top, the final decisions are his, at least legally. These are to be carried out by his hierarchical subordinates upon pain of severance from the service, or, in time of emergency, death.

That such should be the dominant characteristic of military organization is easily explicable. The exigencies of warfare are such that instantaneous coördination is imperative. Failure of the artillery or the tanks or the air force to coöperate with the infantry may lead to the loss of a regiment or of any army. The component parts of the military machine must mesh. The breakdown of one part may lead to the breakdown of the whole. Time is of the essence of things. The uncertainties of voluntary coöperation are inadmissible. The slow moving process of coördination by negotiation is no less unsatisfactory. Coördination must be imposed by command.[1]

Owing in part to the military example and in part to the similarity of their problems, civilian departments of

[1] In making this statement the author is, of course, aware that one of the chief purposes of drill is to habituate recruits not only to the customary activities of army life, but also to stimulate that voluntary coöperation between individual soldiers which cannot be imposed from the top, which frequently reflects the difference between an effective and an ineffective army. This dependence upon voluntary coöperation between individual soldiers, however, in no way, so it seems to the author, detracts from the correctness of the above analysis. The dominant characteristic of the military, as distinct from various forms of coördination in civil administration, is coördination by command communicated down a hierarchical ladder.

government have, by and large, been organized on this same principle. Severance from the service, however, rather than death has, except in some totalitarian states, been the penalty imposed for failure to execute orders.

In the course of decades another principle of administrative organization has developed, that of devolution or operating autonomy. This is best exemplified in the realm of economic organization by the holding-company mode of organization. Instead of concentrating full and final authority in the hands of a single executive, holding companies usually organize their component parts more or less as independent economic units, in many cases directed by independent presidents, immediately responsible to independent boards of trustees. In all such holding companies some measure of coördination is imposed, but the techniques by which it is achieved differ radically. In some situations the board of directors of the top holding company constitutes a majority of the board of directors of each of the operating units. In other cases, the chief executives of the various operating units report directly to the president of the top company. But in any case, devolution rather than integration is the outstanding characteristic of these economic units. The actual administration and management of the various operating organizations is under the direction and supervision of its immediate management. Such coördination as exists, apart from financial and certain technical considerations, is confined to broad questions of business policy or to that limited sphere in which it is thought either that standardization of procedure is imperative or that the overall facilities of the parent organization make possible a contribution of administrative efficiency not otherwise attainable.

Although without question the idiosyncrasies of our partly socialized, partly capitalistic economy, such as the necessity for evading the antitrust laws by creating the appearance of competition, have contributed to this form of development, nevertheless, it is thought to have distinct advantages from a purely administrative point of view.

Briefly summarized these advantages may be said to be: (a) preservation of local initiative and of community contacts; (b) economies of consolidated purchasing; (c) provision of more expert technical services; (d) release of the chief executive from an overburden of routine; and (e) concentration of the top management upon large problems of policy, technical improvements, and operating efficiency.

How far, and in what way, if any, is the holding company principle in any form applicable to government? In an article entitled "Notes on the Theory of Organization," Dr. Luther Gulick, Director of the Institute of Public Administration, offers a negative answer on the grounds that:

(1) There is but one board of directors in the governmental set-up, and a single avenue of democratic responsibility;
(2) The interrelations between the various departments are many and intimate, requiring extensive and continuous coordination;
(3) In government there must be highly developed uniform standards and methods, particularly in finance and personnel; and
(4) There is in government no simple, final measure of successful operation of subsidiaries like the profit and loss statements in business. Supervisory relationships must be intimate and complete, not distant and limited.[2]

Dr. Gulick is quite obviously referring to the application of the principle on a general scale, i.e., the organization of each of the departments into a self-contained unit subordinate to the chief executive only to the extent that a subsidiary corporation is to the top company.

[2] *Papers on the Science of Administration,* edited by Gulick and Urwick (New York, 1937), p. 3.

Although one may question the universality of the assertion that "there is but one board of directors in the governmental set-up, and a single avenue of democratic responsibility," the validity of Dr. Gulick's objections to a wholesale application of the holding-company idea is scarcely to be doubted. Whether these objections are equally valid with reference to certain specific applications of the concept is, however, open to debate.

As a matter of fact, within recent times there has been a growing utilization of the concept both extra- and intradepartmentally. The development of the Tennessee Valley Authority with its semi-independent board of directors represents one variation of the principle as it has been applied extradepartmentally; the creation of a whole series of independent quasi-legislative and quasi-judicial agencies, another. The first partakes in part at least of the nature of geographic decentralization; the second, of functional segmentation.

The application of this principle extradepartmentally is inevitably related to the desirable number and size of the administrative departments; and by virtue of this fact has already been partially discussed. Whether there are exceptional circumstances which justify the utilization of the concept even though it runs counter to any ultimate decision which may be made as to the number and size of the departments will be considered, albeit obliquely, in Chapter VI.

No less pertinent to the question here under consideration is the utilization of the concept intradepartmentally—a phenomenon which is quite as characteristic of administrative development in Great Britain as it is in the United States. In a number of British Ministries, for instance, there are to be found boards, commissions, and individual offices which, although they are under their respective Ministries for purposes of reporting and inspection, are nevertheless not subject to the direction of the Minister nor removable by him. Such, for example, is the Central Electricity Board of the Ministry of Transportation. For a number of years, the Inland Waterways Corporation occupied a practically autonomous position in the Department of War, a position it continues to occupy in the Department of Commerce. The Bituminous Coal Commission, although an integral part of the Department of Interior in so far as its budgeting and general servicing are concerned, was nevertheless "completely independent of departmental control as to its decisions; its members [could] be removed from office by the President only for stated causes." Howard University, although theoretically subject to the supervision of the same department, is practically independent of it. A similar position is occupied by certain of the state universities in relation to their respective departments of education. Although not completely analogous, the Commodity Credit Corporation as well as a number of government-owned corporations likewise occupy positions in the departmental structure not completely under departmental control.

In some respects the relation of these semiautonomous units to their respective departments may be said to be federal in character, i.e., they move in orbits independent of departmental control. The regular structure of the departments themselves, however, cannot be characterized as federal both because the overwhelming majority of their component parts have been integrated with the department upon a unitary or hierarchical basis and because the degree of independence from departmental control granted to specific administrative units varies from agency to agency. In their relation to these units the departments may be viewed as holding companies, rendering to each of the quasi-independent establishments such services and exercising such control as may appear to be suitable, but allowing each agency complete freedom of action in that sphere in which autonomy appears to be a prime requisite for effective work.

The situation which exists in Great Britain, it should be conceded, differs markedly from that which has developed in the United States. This is due to certain fundamental differences in the political structure of the two countries. The simple fact is that a British Minister in charge of any department can, whenever he sees fit—with the consent of his colleagues in the Cabinet—draft a bill, which is certain of passage through Parliament, embodying any suggestions he may have to make either as to the broad lines of public policy which should be followed by any of these semiindependent agencies or as to their administrative procedure. In consequence the members of these quasi-autonomous units are likely to be more receptive to such suggestions as their departmental superiors may make than their American counterparts. This is particularly true if the President and the Congress of the United States are of opposite political persuasions. In point of fact, however, bills of this character are seldom introduced into the British Parliament. And so rare is even the threat of such action that for all practical purposes these various boards and commissions occupy as completely an independent position in the British administrative structure as they do in the American system.

Thus it becomes evident that a limited application of the holding company idea has developed in the civilian departments of both England and the United States, which has already modified quite radically the traditional or hierarchical concept of departmental organization.

But is the concept capable, or likely to be capable, of extended application? To certain students of administration, at any rate, it appears that it is. Indeed, the further development of this concept is looked upon as essentially a compromise between the two lines of reasoning previously analyzed. The argument advanced in the preceding chapter in behalf of the integration of the administrative units of the government into a limited number of large departments, based as it is for the most part upon the assumption that the hierarchical principle will constitute the controlling device of such integration, is recognized to have a very real measure of validity. No less obvious is it that much of the criticism of these large departments and much of the reasoning adduced for the creation of a multiplicity of smaller ones is equally real. The problem then would seem to be the discovery of a method, if possible, to attain the advantages of the large departments but to avoid their disadvantages, to secure the advantages of a multiplicity of small departments but at the same time to escape the difficulties inherent in such a departmental pattern. The answer to the dilemma would appear to be the further application of the holding-company idea to the departmental structure —the development of what, for want of a better term, might be called departments of limited jurisdiction. Such departments would not necessarily be federal in character. Indeed, if a uniform measure of supervisory authority over the several subordinate administrative units were delegated to the holding departments, a considerable measure of the value of the holding-company idea would be lost. Instead, the various subordinate administrative units could be integrated into the departmental structure to just the degree that the peculiar conditions surrounding each unit makes advantageous and no more.

Thus, to draw an illustration from contemporary Washington: if the holding-company concept were adopted, the current proposal to consolidate the Departments of War and Navy into a single Department of National Defense, and the suggestion that the administrative units dealing with transportation be integrated into a great Department of Transportation, would take on a radically different aspect from that which they now possess.

A Department of National Defense might or might not be federal in character. It would certainly embrace two component parts—a Division of War and a Division of Navy. It might also embrace a Division of Military Aviation. Each of these great divisions might be headed by its own secretary and might remain practically autonomous in the conduct of its own internal affairs. Above the three secretaries might be placed a secretary of National Defense. His primary function might be, first, the reception of routine reports from the two or three major divisions as the case might be, and the transmission of such segments of these reports as he might think necessary to the chief executive, and second, the coördination of the overlapping activities of the component parts of the department. In consequence of this he would undoubtedly participate in the work of a Board of National Defense and hold the balance of voting power necessary to break any deadlocks which might develop. Moreover, he might undertake certain military activities now carried on by neither the Department of War nor that of the Navy, or certain functions such as propaganda which are in reality not a technical part of the fighting service.

In a similar manner the several transportation units might be integrated into a single Department of Transportation which might embrace the Inland Waterways Corporation, the Maritime Commission, the Division of Transportation of the Bureau of Foreign and Domestic Commerce, the Coast and Geodetic Survey, the Northern and Northeastern Lakes Survey, the Hydrographic Office, the Naval Observatory, the Bureau of Public Roads, the non-military functions of the Corps of Engineers, the Weather Bureau, the Civil

Aeronautics Authority, the Light House Service, and the Interstate Commerce Commission.

Obviously such a department could not be organized upon a strictly hierarchical basis with all the subordinate administrative units fully subject to departmental direction, supervision, and control. The quasi-judicial character of certain aspects of the work of the Interstate Commerce and Maritime Commissions *ipso facto* precludes any such possibility. It would be possible nevertheless to include these various units within a department organized upon the holding-company concept. In this fashion certain of the units above mentioned whose primary functions are predominantly routine in character might be fully incorporated in the departmental structure, whereas units like the Interstate Commerce and Maritime Commissions whose work is primarily quasi-legislative and quasi-judicial in its nature could be integrated into the departmental structure only to the extent that their housekeeping functions were subordinated to departmental control whereas their major activities might be left completely autonomous.

In this fashion certain of the advantages of large departments could be secured and certain of their disadvantages avoided.

The number of direct and continuous managerial contacts of the chief executive could be radically reduced and thus brought more definitely within his sphere of control. Departmental machinery for the adjudication of jurisdictional disputes could be established and duplication of function or personnel gradually eliminated. Large-scale planning would be possible and a greater degree of coöperation assured. The standardization of procedures could more easily be encouraged where it seems desirable. Interdepartmental and interfunctional conflicts could be reduced. And in consequence of the foregoing, increased efficiency of operation—and economy—might be secured. The breadth of vision of the Cabinet members should be enhanced, and administrative-legislative relationships should be improved. Incidentally, the Departments could act as buffers against undesirable pressure-group influences without necessarily interfering with vitalizing relationships. At the same time, the independence of these smaller administrative units could be adequately preserved. Bottlenecks, administrative or managerial sabotage, and the illusion of self-sufficiency could be avoided. A junior cabinet might be developed, which could be called upon to supplement the discussions of the senior cabinet from a background much richer in a detailed knowledge of the actual operations of their respective administrative units.

But what of Dr. Gulick's four objections? Are they as applicable to the utilization of the holding-company idea intradepartmentally as they are extradepartmentally?

If by his statement, "there is but one board of directors in the governmental set-up, and a single avenue of democratic responsibility," Dr. Gulick refers to the directly elected, policy-determining officials en masse, including both the President and Congress, his statement cannot be successfully controverted. If he means that the lines of responsibility run first to the chief executive, then to the legislature, as they do under the Cabinet system, this is obviously not the case in the United States. Whether it is desirable or not we shall discuss later. The truth is that the Interstate Commerce Commission, the Federal Trade Commission, the United States Maritime Commission, the Securities and Exchange Commission, and the Federal Communications Commission, all report directly to Congress, whereas the National Labor Relations Board reports both to Congress and to the President. Although the President appoints the members of these various bodies, he does so only with the consent of the Senate. And if the Humphrey case holds, he can remove them only upon conditions laid down by Congress. If then Dr. Gulick's statement is intended as an objection to the development of the holding-company idea intra- as well as extra-departmentally, the answer is obvious. In the case of many of the units which might conceivably be included in a department organized on this principle, no single and direct lines of subordination to the chief executive exist anyway. To the extent that these independent quasi-legislative and quasi-judicial bodies are brought into the departmental structure will lines of supervisory authority be instituted. In the case of those other independent administrative units over which the chief executive now has full control, such as the Farm Credit Administration, the Federal Housing Administration, his control will continue. A portion of his potential supervisory authority will be delegated to the heads of the great departments, the balance will remain in *statu quo ante integratum*.

But Dr. Gulick urges "the interrelations between the various departments are many and intimate requiring extensive and continuous coördination" of a character not attainable through the utilization of the holding-company idea. This is undoubtedly true, in so far as it relates to the possibility of treating the various departments as independent operating units of a top holding company. Is it also applicable to the intradepartmental utilization of the concept? Without doubt it is not universally applicable. Thus just as the relation of the various work units within the Bureau of Entomology and Plant Quarantine are so intimate and continuous that hierarchy alone supplies the only sound basis of integration, so do the interrelations of the majority of bureaus within the Department of Agriculture dictate the utilization of this same principle. But it should be noted that limited as is the degree of coördination attainable through the intradepartmental application of the holding-company idea, it is greater by far than that which is possible when these various nonintegrated administrative units are allowed to remain as independent establishments or given the status of small departments. In consequence, the validity of this objection to the development of departments of limited jurisdiction turns entirely upon the functions and purposes which such departments represent.

Dr. Gulick's third objection to the application of the holding-company idea intradepartmentally is not necessarily relevant. It is generally, if not universally, conceded that "in government there must be highly developed uniform standards and methods, particularly in finance and personnel." In so far as the utilization of the holding-company concept intradepartmentally is concerned, its adoption will further rather than interfere with the development of such standards, for by definition one of the major purposes of the development of departments of limited jurisdiction is the centralization of both reporting and servicing, and the standardization of such procedures as may seem desirable without in any way interfering with the vital independence of the semiautonomous operating units. Certainly such standardization is as easy of accomplishment in a limited number of semiintegrated departments as it is in a multiplicity of small ones. It may not, of course, be as thoroughgoing as it would be in a large department organized upon a hierarchical basis, but as has already been indicated, the disadvantages, both administrative and political, frequently more than offset the gains of such complete integration, even assuming the practicability of thoroughgoing consolidation.

Although it is true that "there is in government no simple, final measure of successful operation like the profit and loss statement in business"; and that "supervisory relations must be intimate and complete, not distant and limited," the observation is by no means relevant to any phase of public administration. The choice between the integration of a number of small departments or independent establishments into a limited number of large departments based on the holding-company concept and their continued independence as distinct administrative units is the choice between complete dependence upon the over-all supervision of the chief executive and over-all supervision supplemented by varying degrees of departmental control. In either case there will be "no simple, final measure of successful operation." There will either be the distant and limited supervision of over-all management by the chief executive, or the somewhat more intimate and complete supervision which departmental integration even on this limited scale makes possible, if not inevitable.

Here, too, an even greater degree of supervision could be effected through the medium of a highly integrated hierarchical department, but once again it should be noted that, under certain circumstances at least, the disadvantages of such an organization may much more than offset its advantages, assuming the possibility of such a unification. Attention should be called to the fact that the introduction of the holding-company concept into the departmental structure may result from action either at the top or at the bottom. Thus the integration of the various military agencies of the Federal government into a great Department of National Defense, upon a semiautonomous basis, would constitute one procedure. The attempt made by Premier Blum, a number of years ago, to superimpose six coördinating ministers upon the operating departments of France constitutes another.

In this connection, incidentally, it is pertinent to note that Dr. Gulick himself seems to give tacit consent to the intradepartmental use of the concept, for he himself suggested the grouping of the various departments which go to make up New York City's administrative structure under three or four assistant mayors with the full realization, it may be surmised, that these various departmental groupings would sooner or later evolve into great departments of limited jurisdiction.

Inevitably a number of questions arise as to the practical application of the two concepts. Under what conditions should the several administrative units be fully incorporated in the departmental structure and subjected to departmental supervision and control? When should they be integrated into the departmental structure only to a limited degree? Under these latter circumstances how great should be the measure of autonomy granted? Should the degree of autonomy thus conferred be uniform for all units, or should it vary according to the nature of the function performed?

It is impossible to give a definitive answer to each of the questions thus raised; nevertheless, a number of observations would appear to be relevant. In so far as consolidation involves units of administration whose functions are largely routine in character, the advantages of departmental integration and coördination would appear overwhelmingly and completely to offset any incidental disadvantages which might arise from their incorporation in a departmental structure. Such, however, is not necessarily the case in connection with those agencies whose work is primarily judicial in character. Indeed one might go so far as to say that the very opposite is true. For the experience of the human race would certainly seem to suggest that the judicial function is best performed when the judge is more or less fully protected from political, economic, and administrative pressure. But between these two extremes a whole congeries of problems arises both as to the desirability of including specific administrative units within the departmental structure and as to the degree to which they should be included. Down to date at least, no mathematical formula has been developed for the decisive solution of these problems, nor does it appear likely that the development of any such formula is imminent. Instead, it seems probable that the exact degree of autonomy which should be granted to each operating unit, the work of which is neither purely routine nor quasi-judicial in its nature, will and should be determined by reference to the primary purpose of Congress in establishing the unit, or by reference to some ideal purpose more comprehensive than that of Congress. The more specific criteria upon which the ultimate decisions will be made will also vary widely. In some cases the primary objective of a grant of operating autonomy will be the cutting of the red tape with which routine administration so frequently is hedged; in others, the protection of a unit in the exercise of its quasi-legislative functions.

In other words, the points of reference for determining the conflicts between advocates of administrative hierarchy and administrative devolution do not lie wholly within the field of administrative organization itself. A search for these points of reference leads us into a consideration of the place of the legislature in the whole scheme of government and the degree to which it can or should surrender law-making and policy-determining functions to members of an administrative hierarchy. The quest for efficiency in all branches of administration, however organized, leads not merely to the office of the chief executive. Some of the worst examples of waste, corruption and malfeasance in American history have been furnished by agencies in the administrative hierarchy; while some of the independent agencies bearing closer relations to Congress have far better records. Nor is it to be overlooked that congressional investigations, real or threatened, have been among the most striking correctives making for the proper and efficient discharge of administrative duties. Not until the relations of the executive and the legislature, then, have been explored to the limit and controlling principles fairly well established can the question of hierarchy vs. devolution be determined with a high degree of either administrative or political realism.

V ♦ ♦

CONSIDERATIONS WHICH ENTER INTO
THE CONSTRUCTION OF A DEPARTMENT

AMONG THE DIFFICULT PROBLEMS CONNECTED WITH THE
process of departmentalization is the determination of the
criteria by which the subordinate administrative units should
be grouped together in a departmental structure. At various times and in diverse places a multiplicity of factors
have entered into decisions. For the most part, however,
these factors fall into a series of categories from which a
limited number of generalizations have been drawn. As a
result of these generalizations it is commonly asserted that
the process of departmentalization rests upon four major
concepts of organization: (1) function; (2) work processes;
(3) clientele; and (4) territory.

On the surface the fundamental character of these several modes of organization may seem to be self-evident,
yet such is far from the case. Before turning to the question of their application, it might be well, consequently, to
examine the nature of the concepts themselves.

The difficulty of so defining these concepts as to render
them capable of automatic application is strikingly revealed
in connection with the "principle" of functionalism itself.
The term is usually thought to denote the grouping together
in a departmental organization of those subordinate administrative units which are dedicated to the same or similar
purposes—the solution of the same or similar problems.
Upon the basis of this hypothesis, the several military units

concerned with land defense are commonly grouped together in a Department of War; the naval units in a Department of Navy.

This definition is perfectly satisfactory as far as it goes, but unfortunately it does little more than indicate the dominant characteristic of the concept. Its exact boundaries remain to be delineated. The difficulties inherent in this definition can, perhaps, best be indicated by a series of questions.

Should the various military and naval units of the government be grouped together in separate military and naval establishments as suggested previously? Or should they be integrated into a single Department of National Defense? Both modes of organization would, in the light of the definition given above, be functional in character. In consequence, the mere enunciation of a general "principle of administration" is of little or no help in settling the problem.

Still another aspect of the definition which gives rise to uncertainty is the difficulty of determining the purpose to which the several administrative units are actually dedicated. What, for example, is the primary purpose of the German system of transport, civil or military? Is it the same in time of war as it is in time of peace? Obviously not. In time of war the transportation system of Germany— or for that matter of any other country—is an integral part of the system of national defense. Should it therefore, along with the army, navy, and air force be consolidated with the Ministry of National Defense? Or should it be permitted to retain an autonomous position? What should be done in time of peace? Would the conclusions relative to the proper situs of these agencies as a result of a study of the German situation be equally applicable to the United States?

The answers to these questions will not be discovered by a microscopic analysis of the definition given above. Instead they will be found by an investigation of the political, economic, administrative and military conditions surrounding each given situation. One answer might be given in time of war; another, in time of peace. One solution might be proper for the German Reich, another for the United States. Nevertheless, until we have ascertained the fundamental purposes to which the activities of the several subordinate administrative units have been directed, little or no progress can be made in the application of the concept. To give meaning to the concept these purposes must be discovered.

At times the objectives to which the several administrative units are directed are clearly set forth in the fundamental law of the land. Illustrations of this fact can be found in the constitution of practically every state in the American union. More frequently, however, they are to be found in legislative enactments, administrative decrees and court decisions; often as in the event of war, they are to be found in the nature of the situation itself. Any attempt to apply the concept of functionalism to a concrete situation consequently necessitates not merely a survey of the administrative activities of the several units of administration but an examination of the actions of constituent assemblies, legislative and judicial bodies as well. For only after an analysis of the decisions of all the policy-determining bodies directly or indirectly concerned with the activities of the several administrative units is it possible to arrive at the underlying legislative intent. And only after the discovery of the legislative intent in relation to the specific situations under discussion is it possible to implement the meaning of the concept to the point of practical applicability.

No less disconcerting than the inadequacy of the definition, as it has been indicated in the paragraphs immediately preceding, is the difficulty—under certain circumstances at least—of differentiating some of these organizational concepts from others. Superficially the distinction between them is clear. Thus, as has already been pointed out, departmentalization according to function has been defined as the grouping of subordinate administrative units in a departmental pattern upon the basis of the underlying purpose to which they have each been dedicated. Departmentalization according to work processes seems even more simple. It has as its primary *raison d'être* the bringing together in a single department of those who have had similar professional training or who make use of the same or similar equipment. Departmentalization upon the basis of clientele is also apparently self-explanatory, and should result in the concentration in a single department of those subordinate administrative units which are designed to serve some particular segment of the body politic.

Without question each of these definitions reveals the essential qualities of the mode of organization it purports to define. Undoubtedly also, on the basis of these definitions it is possible to characterize many of the administrative departments as they exist in the various countries in the world today. No less indubitable is it, however, that these definitions fail to delineate clearly the boundaries between the several concepts themselves, and are in consequence responsible for a considerable measure of the obscurity and confusion which characterizes much of the abstract discussion of the subject.

The point may be clarified by means of illustration. The primary object of the Department of War is the military defense of the nation. It is, in consequence, quite evidently organized upon a functional basis. Under its aegis, there has been brought together a tremendous personnel with similar professional training who make use of similar equipment. But this by definition is organization upon the basis of another concept—work processes. The question inevitably arises: Upon what basis is the Department of War actually organized? The answer in this case is reasonably clear—and in any case does not make much difference. The paramount consideration which has governed the development of the department has been that of function or purpose at least in the minds of fundamental thinkers as distinguished from routineers—everything else has been incidental.

Such, however, is not the case in connection with the oft-proposed Department of Public Works. Ostensibly such a department might be organized around a single purpose: the construction of all such public works as the policy-determining body might authorize. An incidental result of the development of such a department would be the concentration in a single department of the vast majority of the civilian engineering staffs now employed by the government. Would the fact that such a unit was called a Department of Public Works justify its characterization as a functionally organized department? What if the title of such a department were changed to that of Engineering? Obviously the mere nomenclature of the department would not be decisive in the matter. It would be necessary to investigate the internal organization of the department to discover whether the department was primarily oriented to the solution of a congeries of problems in all their ramifications or whether its *raison d'être* was the economies and efficiencies which might be effected through the closer integration of the engineering activities of the administration. In point of fact both considerations might well play a part in the creation of such an administrative agency.

The illustration clearly indicates the shadowy line which delineates the concepts of function and process.

No less difficult is it, on occasion, to distinguish between the concept of functionalism and that of clientele. In this connection passing reference may be made to the Department of Agriculture, which is at one and the same time devoted to the administration of agricultural legislation designed to solve the nation's agricultural problems, and to the service of a major segment of the country's population. So closely interrelated are these motifs that it is often impossible to disentangle them in the departmental organization. The fact should, of course, be noted that the services rendered to the agricultural community are often in themselves ways and means of solving the country's agricultural problems. Nevertheless, the rendering of services to this segment of our population in connection with problems not peculiarly agricultural in character such as those rendered by the Bureau of Home Economics suggests that the concept of clientele rather than function has on occasion dominated in specific operations of the department. In any event an analysis of the Department of Agriculture will quickly reveal that the line of demarcation between the concept of function and that of clientele is at times just as hazy as that which separates the concept of function from that of work processes.

In the light of this analysis the question inevitably arises as to the utility of discussing such ill-defined and poorly delineated concepts in the abstract.

The question implies a far greater degree of confusion than actually exists. For although it must be conceded that the generally accepted definitions are somewhat unsatisfactory both in their failure to supply concrete criteria as to their applicability and in the twilight zones which characterize their boundaries, there is, nevertheless, connected with each of these concepts, a real core of meaning. Thus, although these generalizations scarcely deserve the characterization of "principles of administration," they must nevertheless be given a prominent place among the factors which must be weighed in the construction of a departmental organization.

Under what conditions should emphasis be laid upon one of these considerations rather than another? In what circumstances should similarity of purpose or function dominate the development of a departmental structure? When are the services rendered to a particular segment of the body politic of paramount importance? What weight, if any, should be given to factors of professional advantage or technical efficiency? How significant is the mere matter of place or territory? These are weighty matters in the creation of a departmental structure and as such deserve extended consideration.

In connection with any analysis of these several concepts, however, a preliminary caution should be emphasized. No one has ever advocated the construction of departments solely upon the basis of function, or work processes, or clientele or territory. Instead, in the very nature of things, functional, technical, clientele, and territorial factors enter into the construction and operation of all national or large-area departments. Such considerations vary from division of work to division of work, and practice and common sense take them into account as existing departmental organizations demonstrate. Back of all technical considerations, however, lie large questions of national policy and purpose which have a bearing upon present practices and proposed innovations. Given a particular set of assumptions respecting public policy—e.g., the desirability of maintaining constitutional government, the normal judicial processes, legislative control over the administration, etc.—the problem then is the emphasis which should be laid upon one relevancy rather than another, i.e., function, clientele, etc., in a given social context and the particular devices which can be adopted to offset any disadvantages to efficiency accruing from a given emphasis.

Such being the case, the discussion which follows is not intended to lead the reader to a conclusion as to the superiority of one mode of organization over another at all times and in all places. Nor is it designed to indicate that any one concept is sufficient to constitute in and of itself an adequate basis of departmental organization—although it may be conceded that under certain circumstances at least one or other of these hypotheses is very frequently the dominant principle in the construction of a department. Instead, it is hoped that the analysis of these various concepts will produce in the reader's mind an awareness of the factors which at a given time and place were thought worthy of serious consideration.

FUNCTION

The most widely utilized basis of departmental integration is that of function or purpose. In whole or in part the Departments of State, War, Navy, Post Office, Agriculture, Commerce, Labor, and Treasury in the United States rest upon this foundation. This is also true of the Ministries of National Defense and War, Navy, Air, Education, Foreign Affairs, Finance, Posts, Telegraph, and Telephone, etc., in France; and the Ministries of Foreign Affairs, Finance, War, Navy, Aeronautics, and Education in Italy. Illustrations might similarly be drawn from Great Britain, Germany, or Russia. The simple fact is that a considerable number of departments, perhaps a majority, in every major unit of government in the world are dominated to some degree by this principle.

Possibly the greatest advantage which this basis of departmental organization possesses is the fact that it expedites the performance of a given task, the solution of a given problem.

Obviously if all the administrative units concerned with a particular job are integrated in a single department, subject to the direction of a single supervisory officer, the task ought to be accomplished more expeditiously than if these same administrative units are scattered hither and yon throughout the administration. No energy need be wasted working out agreements with other branches of the administration. Interdepartmental frictions can be minimized. Priorities can be decided upon the needs of the situation rather than upon the basis of departmental loyalties. The proper timing of the activities of the various administrative units involved can be worked out. Orders can be issued and action assured.

The point can be made clearer, perhaps, through the use of an illustration. It would seem axiomatic, for example, that the various military units connected with land operations—the General Staff, Office of the Adjutant General, Inspector General, Judge Advocate General, Quartermaster General, Surgeon General, Engineers, Ordnance, Signal Officer, Air Corps, Field Artillery, Coast Artillery, Infantry, etc.—should be concentrated in a single department rather than scattered throughout the administrative structure. The primary objective of these military forces is to meet, check, and defeat the enemy. Supplies and munitions must arrive at a given place at a given time. The air corps must warn of the massing of enemy troops. Tanks and artillery must support the infantry when their support is needed. In other words, the machinery must exist for an almost instantaneous coördination of the activities of all the military units engaged in active warfare.

This is only possible if these various and sundry units have been integrated into a single department under a unified command. To scatter these units among the civilian departments, thus necessitating not only a tremendous waste of time in the negotiation of interdepartmental agreements at some crucial moment, or worse still, making possible inter·

departmental friction and deadlock, would be so inconceivably fantastic that in fact it is never done. All active military units connected with land warfare are everywhere component parts of a single Department of War or of National Defense. Any alternative form of organization would be almost synonymous with military suicide.

Although the necessity for unity of action is most strikingly illustrated in connection with military and naval operations, it is often equally desirable in other fields. If a serious attempt is to be made to solve our agricultural problems, for example, it is imperative that the various administrative units whose work impinges directly upon the solution of these problems should be subjected to centralized direction and control. If it is to work effectively, a department of education, obviously, must have under its jurisdiction not merely the school teachers and administrators, but the janitors, carpenters, electricians, school-bus operators, and anyone else whose work is an integral part of the educational system.

As we have already indicated, the failure to integrate functionally the various units of the Federal Government of the United States handling transportation has up to the present rendered exceedingly difficult, if not impossible, the development of any comprehensive, coördinated plan in regard to the transportation system of the United States—a plan which, by virtue of the fact that the government has been dealing with various aspects of the problem for more than seventy-five years, should have been worked out long ago.

But nothing of the sort has happened. Instead, within recent years, numerous plans, more or less partial and conflicting, have emerged from various agencies of the Federal government. For years the Senate Committee on Interstate Commerce has been investigating railway financing and operations; the Interstate Commerce Committee of the

House of Representatives has been conducting inquiries of its own. In 1934 Congress created the office of Coördinator of Transportation, to which Joseph B. Eastman was appointed, and instructed him to prepare a report on proposals for coping with the evident crisis in the railway world. In 1935 Mr. Eastman made a comprehensive and systematic set of plans for dealing with the railways, but no action was taken on his proposals. Meanwhile new federal agencies have been set up in connection with the regulation of water, air, and motor transportation, and conferences on the subject of transportation have been held in the White House. After many years of investigation, legislation, and discussion, disturbances in the realm of transportation are as confusing as ever, if not more so.

Integration by function thus not only insures unity of action but it contributes considerably to a more completely rounded consideration of all aspects of a given problem or congeries of problems than is likely under any other form of organization.

Another advantage inherent in the integration of the subordinate administrative units of government upon the basis of purpose is that this mode of departmentalization contributes somewhat to a reduction of the degree of overlapping and duplication which otherwise appears to be inevitable.

Owing to the fact that the United States Employment Service, the Social Security Board, the Public Works Administration, and the Works Progress Administration (now Work Projects Administration) were formerly independent units rather than integral parts of a single agency dedicated to the solution of the unemployment problem, friction rather than coöperation has more than once characterized their relationships. Similarly, only continuous consultation and an attitude of the utmost willingness to coöperate and to accommodate prevented the Social Security Board and the Department of Labor from unnecessarily duplicating each other's statistical services.

Although the activities of the United States Conciliation Service and the National Labor Relations Board do not at the moment duplicate each other specifically, it seems fairly clear that both units may, in the course of years, build up professional staffs larger than their joint needs. The fact that the various health services of the government have been scattered among a number of administrative agencies has given rise to mutual recrimination and the charge of needless duplication—a situation which has only recently been corrected by the efforts of the Interdepartmental Committee and by the Administrative Reorganization of 1939.

In each of these situations, had the various administrative units been concentrated under the aegis of a single administrative department, it is very probable that the duplication of facilities, personnel, and activities would have been easily ironed out. The point should not be too strongly emphasized, however. Although it is true that integration according to function usually leads to the minimization of certain types of duplication and overlapping, nevertheless, as we shall see shortly, this form of organization is itself, to some slight degree at any rate, productive of these same undesirable results.

Equally advantageous, in the opinion of certain students of public administration at any rate, is the fact that integration according to function conforms best with "the objectives of government as they are recognized and understood by the public. The public sees the end result and cannot understand the methodology. It can therefore express its approval or disapproval with less confusion and more effectiveness regarding major purposes than it can regarding the processes." [1] This might be expressed in other terms. Since the public is primarily interested in the solution of particular problems or the discharge of certain public duties, rather than in the administrative techniques or procedures by which the solutions are worked out or duties discharged, the grouping of the various administrative units in a series of departments organized around the operations in a given field of human endeavor is distinctly advantageous in that, to some extent at least, it fixes the responsibility for performances, and in so doing focuses public attention upon the responsible officials. Under some circumstances it may marshal the support of a powerful segment of the community behind the administrative units involved in working out a problem or conducting given operations. Such, for example, has been the position of the Department of Agriculture both in connection with the formulation of its plans for crop control and in their administration. Alternatively this procedure may concentrate such a battery of criticism on a departmental program as to cause its modification or even abandonment.

The simple fact is that integration according to function radically reduces the number of situations in which administrative officials can engage in the time-honored pastime of "buck-passing." This, it should be remarked parenthetically, is not an exclusive attribute of integration on the basis of function since organization on the basis of clientele frequently produces a similar result.

No less important in the minds of many observers is the influence which this simplification of the machinery of government may be expected to exert in connection with the less spectacular but more frequent day-to-day relations existing between the administration and particular seg-

[1] *Papers on the Science of Administration*, edited by Gulick and Urwick (New York, 1937), p. 22.

ments of the body politic over the interpretation of the detail of various statutes. Thus the manufacturer who is both annoyed and embarrassed by the fact that diverse information called for by the Bureau of Internal Revenue and the Bureau of Customs unnecessarily complicates the keeping of his books can appeal the whole question to the Treasury with the full knowledge that the problem can be settled intradepartmentally, and that it will not have to undergo the slow and tedious process of interdepartmental negotiation or be bogged down in a morass of interdepartmental jealousy and negligence. The manufacturers who worked out trade practices with the approval of the National Recovery Administration knew they did not have to fear a suit for the violation of the antitrust laws initiated by the Federal Trade Commission. Under the Reorganization of 1939 the applicant for rural relief does not have to wander from the Resettlement Administration to the Farm Credit Administration and back again in an endeavor to find the exact category into which he fits.

In short, the integration of the subordinate administrative units of government into a series of functional departments simplifies the relations of the administration to the public, through the creation of the machinery required for the adjudication of an unnecessary duplication of bureaucratic demands, through a clear-cut delineation of the functions of the subordinate units and the establishment of a method of intradepartmental clearance, and last, but by no means least, through the departmental determination of all broad questions of policy and the elimination or at least minimization of conflicting administrative actions.

Yet, despite the advantages inherent in the principle of functionalism as a basis of departmental integration, a number of defects are clearly apparent.

The first is the difficulty of differentiating the illusion of functionalism from the reality thereof. For example, in connection with the recent proposal to change the name of the Department of Interior to the Department of Conservation on the ground that the latter name more accurately describes its purpose, the question inevitably arises: conservation of what? Of our territorial boundaries? The Departments of State, War, and Navy have, presumably, some slight interest in the question. Of our human resources? The Departments of Labor, Agriculture, and Commerce might all insist that such a department would encompass many, if not all, of their activities. Of our natural resources? The Department of Agriculture has already protested, and protested rather vigorously, that the effective utilization of agricultural lands is part and parcel of any program dedicated to the conservation of our natural resources.

In other words, the term functionalism is, seemingly, capable of such broad interpretation, or misinterpretation, that it can be used to justify the creation of a department which would encompass the entire government. Needless to say, in this sense the concept of functionalism is totally valueless as a basis of departmental integration.

But the difficulty of differentiating the illusion from the reality of functionalism does not end here. If it did the task would be relatively simple. The real problem is presented in such suggestions as the proposed consolidation of the Departments of War and Navy into a Department of National Defense, already referred to in pages preceding; the integration of the health, education and welfare units into a Department of Public Welfare; or alternatively, the combination of the labor, social security, and welfare units into a single Department of Social Affairs. Which suggestion truly embodies the principle of organization according to function?

The danger of the acceptance of the illusion of integration for the reality thereof lies in the neglect or suppression of certain aspects of the department's work. Thus, despite the arguments advanced earlier that any one whose work is intimately related with the educational system should be under the aegis of a department of education, it is frequently asserted that "medical work with children when established under the department of education as a division is less likely to receive encouragement than it would if independently established in the health department, because after all the department of education is primarily interested in schools and has its own great needs and problems." [2] Similarly fear has been expressed by the medical profession lest the incorporation of the United States Public Health Service in a Department of Public Welfare should lead to its neglect by a welfare-minded head of department.[3] In like fashion it is urged that the proposal to create a great Department of Finance which would encompass within its jurisdiction the Reconstruction Finance Corporation, the Home Loan Bank Board, and the Farm Credit Administration rests upon the illusion of functionalism rather than reality itself. And that if it were acted upon, it might enable a treasury-minded Secretary of Finance, whose primary concern might be to reduce the burden imposed on the taxpayers, to sabotage the various units subjected to his control in their attempts to work out the exceedingly complicated credit problems assigned to them.

Whatever success or lack of success may result from the

[2] *Papers on the Science of Administration,* p. 22.

[3] It may well be, of course, that the real fear of the medical practitioners who advance this line of reasoning is the expansion of public-health service; their rationalization, nevertheless, is worth noting.

attempt to differentiate the illusion of functionalism from the reality thereof, it is a curious paradox that functionalism is conducive to departmental duplication in connection with certain types of supplementary services. For example, both the Department of War and the Department of the Navy insist on maintaining certain auxiliary forces under their own immediate command, although many of them might, so it is asserted, be supplied more efficiently by the sister service. Thus, attached to the Navy is the Marine Corps, a military unit which is comparable in almost every particular to the land forces maintained by the Department of War. The Department of War in its turn operates a number of its own vessels for the purpose of facilitating the movement of troops and supplies. Each of the two services, moreover, maintains its own air force. Such duplication, needless to say, is not confined to the fighting forces, but is discernible in the civilian departments as well.

For the most part, however, this duplication occurs in connection with incidental and supplementary services. And is of importance largely as an aspect of the personnel problem in as much as the incidental character of the work involved frequently makes impossible the most effective utilization of either personnel or equipment. This is likely to be the case for two reasons: the limited amount of auxiliary work frequently does not justify the maintenance of the most up-to-date and expensive equipment, and the limited career offered by these supplementary services rarely attracts or retains individuals of distinct ability. The work of a medical officer attached to the township or county schools, for example, will rarely justify the laboratory or clinical facilities available to the medical officers attached to the local board of health or municipal hospital. Moreover, except in a very large school system, there is little or no professional advancement possible for the medical officers commensurate with that offered the school teachers or educational administrators. The result frequently is that the office is filled by a youngster who expects to transfer to another field of activity as soon as the opportunity arises, a third rater who feels that the limitations of the career offered approximate the limits of his ability, or by a local practitioner who looks upon the income from the work as an incidental supplement to his private income and whose major interest lies elsewhere.

A similar situation existed for a long time in connection with the public health offices attached to the Office of Indian Affairs, although here the isolated character of the work accentuated the defects inherent in this form of organization. Needless to say, the undesirable consequences which flow from the development of a series of supplementary service units in departments which are organized upon the basis of function have not been confined to the medical aspects of the work. Indeed, except in those unique situations in which an effort has been made to work out a system of personal transfers transcending departmental lines, a similar condition exists in most of the auxiliary units attached to departments integrated upon the basis of function.

This duplication, however, should not be overstressed. As already indicated, it occurs chiefly in connection with the incidental and auxiliary services, and is, in any final evaluation of the concept of functionalism, likely to be relatively unimportant.

More disadvantageous in its effects upon departmental operations is the fact that the grouping of the subordinate administrative units into a series of departments upon the basis of function frequently produces an attitude of self-sufficiency on the part of the departmental managers which results both in administrative astigmatism and an unwillingness to coöperate with other departments. The mere fact that the departmental managers have under their direction all of the units of government directly concerned with performances and the solution of the problems to which the department is dedicated is frequently conducive to the development of a departmental bias or emphasis likely to interfere with the capacity of the departmental managers to view their affairs in a broad perspective. For instance, the Department of Agriculture is very apt to think of the development of our water resources largely from the angle of soil erosion, with little or no regard for the utilization of those resources either from the point of view of power or of navigation. Similarly, the creation of a Department of Public Utilities would entail the risk that the development of our water resources would be viewed essentially as a problem of power, rather than one of navigation or soil erosion. Still another bias would in all probability characterize the proposed Department of Transportation which might well view the development of our river systems exclusively from the point of view of their potentialities as arteries of commerce.

The defects inherent in the functional organization have, in a measure at least, been responsible for the creation of a number of multifunctional agencies, among which the Office of Indian Affairs and the Tennessee Valley Authority constitute two outstanding examples.

Unquestionably the grouping of the subordinate administrative units into a series of departments upon a functional basis all too often leads to such a degree of self-sufficiency that the departmental managers appear to view the world through an inverted telescope. The departmental aspects of each problem are concentrated upon; the broader aspects neglected. A further disadvantage which organization according to function produces at times is, as already indicated, an unwillingness to coöperate with other departments, or, at the least, an insistence upon the priority of all departmental obligations.

For example, it would appear to be obvious that the fundamental task of the federal government's placement service during the depression was to get the unemployed to work, whether on public works, works progress projects, or in private industry; but the United States Employment Service insisted that its primary duty was to its Department —that its existing relationship to employers would be greatly disturbed if it were to undertake the placement of the unemployed on any other basis than their relative merits—that it could not conscientiously subscribe, consequently, to the thesis that every employable man was entitled to a job. The result, as we have already discovered, was a prolonged conflict between the United States Employment Service and the Works Progress Administration, and, in a number of states, at least, a temporary break between them.

This experience on the part of the Works Progress Administration was by no means unique. Almost continuously the W.P.A. had difficulty in preventing the various departments and other administrative units organized upon a functional basis from diverting money which had been appropriated for the purpose of providing the unemployed with jobs to the purchase or hire of labor-saving machinery. From the point of view of these functionally organized units the important thing was getting their tasks performed, the problems solved. The necessity of providing a maximum number of jobs for the unemployed was in their opinion an unwelcome irritation. Only the fact that the Works Progress Administration had in most cases the final decision in the allocation of tremendous sums of money enabled it to exert sufficient authority to compel coöperation.

Scarcely less deleterious than any of the disadvantages thus far cited in its influence upon the process of administration is the fact that the rigid application of the principle of functionalism to the administrative structure unnecessarily complicates the number of contacts between the public and the government. If the Indian Bureau, for example, were segmented into its constituent parts, and the various parts were allocated to a series of functional departments, a portion of its activities would go to the Treasury, another portion to a Department of Public Welfare, a third, to the Department of Agriculture, and the remaining activities here, there, and elsewhere. In so far as "the poor Indian" is concerned, the result would be confusion thrice confounded. It would be necessary for each individual Indian to take up his various and sundry problems with a multiplicity of governmental agencies, instead of dealing with a single office. Similarly, if the Veterans Administration were reorganized on the basis of function, its diverse activities would be scattered among a number of departments. Certain aspects of its work would be assigned to the Treasury, and others to a Department of Public Welfare; the balance would be divided among administrative subdivisions in still other parts of the departmental structure. The inevitable consequence would be a multiplication of the offices through which the veteran would of necessity transact his business. Whether the advantages which are attainable through a rigid application of the principle of functionalism would more than offset the inconveniences which would result is certainly controversial.

A still further result of a universal application of the functional principle would be the dismissal from consideration of a whole congeries of political factors which in a democracy certainly cannot be overlooked.

PROCESS

An alternative method of departmental integration is on the basis of work processes, whether dictated by personnel or equipment. Thus there would be brought together in a single department all those who practice a given or related profession, e.g., engineering, teaching, medicine, law, military or naval science, or who make use of similar complicated equipment. The adoption of this principle, needless to say, would necessitate a radical shift in the foci of many departments as they are organized today. A Department of Health would include all doctors, and all nurses, bacteriologists, psychologists, etc., as well. Not only would it handle all the general public-health work for the government but the health services now carried on by the schools and the various welfare units; and, if the principle were vigorously applied, the medical work of the army and navy would similarly fall within its jurisdiction. Members of the legal profession would be attached to the Department of Justice or, as it might more accurately be called, the Department of Law, and detailed therefrom to specific assignments. Similarly, the engineers would have their headquarters in a Department of Engineering and would likewise be assigned to other units as the need arose. Here, too, if the principle were pushed to its logical conclusion, the engineering work of the army and navy might conceivably be handled by a detail from the Department of Engineering.

This principle of organization, it is asserted, is conducive to "the maximum utilization of up-to-date technical skill, and by bringing together in a single office a large amount of each kind of work (technologically measured) makes it possible in each case to make use of the most effective divisions of work and specialization." [4] Thus if school doctors

[4] *Papers on the Science of Administration,* p. 23.

were attached to the health department instead of the Department of Education, they would be in constant touch with their professional colleagues and should in consequence be the recipients of professional stimuli not otherwise probable. Moreover, they would have access to much better equipped laboratories than are otherwise available. Finally, the increased volume of medical work canalized to a Department of Health from all sources would make possible an otherwise unattainable degree of specialization within the Department both in connection with diagnosis, prevention, and treatment.

The utilization of this basis of departmental integration would also make possible a considerable measure of economy both as a result of a more extensive use of labor-saving machinery and as a result of mass production. Thus the concentration of all printing in the hands of the Government Printing Office has undoubtedly avoided the duplication not only of linotype machines and printing presses by each of the departments but has also radically reduced a duplication of personnel. In this vein, the President's Committee on Administrative Management argued that the concentration of all engineering units now maintained by the government into a single Department of Public Works would materially lessen the existing duplication of the very expensive construction machinery made inevitable by the present organization of engineering work. At the moment much of this machinery is used only upon a part-time basis.

Organization by process, it is insisted furthermore, makes possible much more effective coördination in all of the technical and skilled work of an enterprise, "because all of those engaged in any field are brought together under the same supervision instead of being scattered in the several departments as is the case when organization is based upon some other principle." [5] Such, for example, has been the heart of the argument in behalf of the centralization of the statistical work now being carried on by the functionalized departments. The Central Statistical Board, it should be remarked parenthetically, was essentially a compromise between concentration upon the basis of process and the decentralization which is necessary under a functionalized departmental system.[6] In similar fashion, it is argued, the concentration of all legal talent in a single department, whether of Justice or of Law, would *ipso facto* produce more careful legal work and certainly a greater degree of uniformity in the preparation of executive orders, departmental regulations, and drafts of proposed legislation.

Organization by process, it is contended, greatly facilitates cost analyses in the several fields and therefore makes more readily available comparative data respecting unit costs. In consequence, it affords a useful basis for the organization of certain particular services such as budgeting, accounting, purchasing, etc., even when it is not utilized throughout the entire administrative field.

Perhaps the strongest argument in behalf of departmentalization on this basis, however, is the fact that in many respects at least it is best adapted to the development of a career service for government employees, especially if the

[5] *Ibid.*, p. 24.

[6] The organization of the Central Statistical Board illustrates incidentally the artificiality which characterizes discussions of administrative "principles." The reader should be warned once again of the exceedingly limited value of an analysis of these concepts in the abstract. It is useful, as has been pointed out previously, only in calling attention to considerations which at some given time and place have been deemed worthy of evaluation. At no time and in no place has any department ever been constructed upon the basis of one of these concepts alone. Instead all departments rest upon that combination of and compromise between these various concepts which the exigencies of time and place have dictated.

present basis of recruitment, with its strongly marked vocational element, continues. In a departmental organization based upon process, the school doctor need not feel that he is in a dead end professionally. If the Department of Health is properly organized, he can clearly see the rungs of the ladder up which he may make a professional ascent. The engineer attached to the Office of Education need not feel that he is merely an incident in the educational system. The path to professional advancement is clearly marked within a Department of Public Works. Professional advancement is, of course, possible, no matter how the departments are organized, by transfer from one department to another. But such transfers are often slightly less difficult than the transfer to private employment. At the present time, there is no more guarantee that an engineering task well done in the Department of Agriculture will lead to advancement in one of the major engineering units of the government than that it will attract the attention of private employers. Organization by process at least ensures the supervision of each professional task by a superior officer more nearly competent to pass upon the quality of its execution than does any other form of departmental organization. And, if the department is properly organized and administered, it should be conducive to promotion upon a more equitable basis than might otherwise be the case.

Despite the very real economies and operating efficiencies which may accrue from the grouping of the subordinate administrative units into departments upon the basis of process, conflicts and frictions are also inherent in the procedure.

In the first place, if this principle were applied universally or even generally, the burden of coördination imposed upon the chief executive in any large system would be beyond his physical and mental capacity. As Dr. Gulick has pointed out, "purpose departments must be coördinated so that they will not conflict but will work shoulder to shoulder. But whether they do, or do not, the individual major purposes will be accomplished to a considerable extent and a failure in any service is limited in its effect to that service. Process departments must be coördinated not only to prevent conflicts, but also to guarantee positive coöperation. They must work hand in hand. They must also time their work so that it will fit together, a factor of lesser significance in the purpose departments. A failure in one process affects the whole enterprise, and a failure to coördinate one process division may destroy the effectiveness of all of the work that is being done." [7]

Recurring to an illustration used earlier, the activities of the commissary, the engineering units, the medical corps, the office of ordnance, etc., simply must be coördinated with those of the infantry, tanks, and artillery, or else an entire campaign may be lost. The rigid utilization of process as a basis of departmental organization would allocate certain of these units to positions in the administrative structure outside the Department of War. In the event of hostilities, this would necessitate a rapidity of interdepartmental coordination which would in all probability be unattainable. The sheer logic of necessity would force a grouping of these units immediately under the chief executive. The upshot would be a hastily improvised Department of National Defense organized upon a functional basis. But the advantages of traditional interdepartmental relations between the military units would be lost.

Although, as has been said previously, the time element in the military situation is, perhaps, more imperative than it is in any other, nevertheless it is not lacking elsewhere.

[7] *Papers on the Science of Administration*, p. 25.

In a slum-clearance project, for example, the task of inter-departmental coördination might well involve the legal department in connection with the acquisition of title to ground, architects and engineers to prepare plans, lawyers to pass on the form of contracts, financial officers to disburse money and to scrutinize accounts, and other special agents. If any one of the departments to which these various activities have been allocated fails to act at the requisite time, or refuses to act, the work of the other departments is inevitably delayed, or alternatively, the entire project may have to be abandoned.

Not even the most vigorous proponents of the concept of organization according to process, it should be noted parenthetically, believe that the concept is capable of universal application. No one, for example, has ever seriously proposed a Department of Stenography or Carpentry or Clock Winding. To do so would be preposterous. The multiplication of departments in direct ratio to the number of special processes used in government service could result only in administrative chaos. Although a knowledge of stenography, for example, is highly desirable for a stenographer, familiarity with the work being done is almost as important.

To a considerable extent this is also true of the more highly professionalized services. Thus the proposal that all lawyers in the government service be attached to a central Department of Law and detailed therefrom as need arises totally overlooks the fact that intimacy with the problems involved is frequently as vital to the satisfactory handling of legal matters as is legal training itself. There is an immense difference, for example, in the character of the legal work involved in connection with the Federal Home Loan Bank Board, the Department of Treasury, and the Department of State. This is most strikingly illustrated, perhaps, by the fact that the average law school offers separate courses on real-estate law, income-tax law, and international law, and that law-school professors dedicate the major portions of their lives to specialization in these respective fields.

The maximum utilization of up-to-date skill, incidentally, is not an inevitable concomitant of organization according to process. Indeed, the health officers assigned to school work, or the naval officers detailed to transport service, or the lawyers allocated to the Department of Interior may either be youngsters just beginning their professional careers assigned to these various posts for the simple reason that from the point of view of the department as a whole they appear to be relatively unimportant, or they may be misfits whom the heads of the various departments have been too tenderhearted to discharge. A system of detail from the process departments to subsidiary services may actually enable the head of each of these various departments to keep their youngsters employed while they are gaining maturity and experience in aspects of the administration in which he, the department head, is least interested, or alternatively, to locate misfits in positions in which from his point of view they will do the least harm. In both cases, however, the result may be inefficiency in so far as the administration of these subsidiary functions is concerned.

A further criticism brought against this method of organization is that it tends to make means more important than ends. This may easily result in the development of a red-tape bureaucracy. Even today there are "accountants who think that the only reason for running a government is the keeping of books." And one sometimes suspects that many of the complicated aspects of legal procedure are due to the reverence of the legal profession for form rather than for content. Organization according to process would, it is asserted, definitely accentuate the influence of the ritualists.

Moreover, such a pattern of organization is weighted on

the side of financial extravagance. The fact that the Bureau of Reclamation has been guided by engineers rather than by agriculturalists has, so it is charged, been partly if not primarily responsible for the development of a number of reclamation projects which have not been self-sustaining.[8] Errors have been made, so the criticism runs, which could not conceivably have been committed had the Bureau been subject to the supervision of a department fundamentally concerned with the problem of agriculture, and only incidentally interested in keeping its staff of engineers employed. This, it is argued, is the great danger in creating a Department of Engineering or Public Works. The head of such a department, so it is claimed, will feel morally obligated to keep his staff employed, and will, in consequence, countenance the construction of engineering projects another department head might disapprove.

It is appropriate here to point out that the argument relative to a more efficacious utilization of equipment and machinery may in fact turn out to be entirely fallacious. In connection with the recent inquiry into the possibility of the administrative reorganization of the federal government, the investigators for the Brookings Institution concluded that the expense of shipping the heavy engineering machinery from one section of the country to another would much more than offset any savings which might be affected by its greater interdepartmental use.

Another undesirable consequence which frequently flows from this mode of departmental organization is the development of an attitude of professional arrogance on the part of the departmental managers and an irritation at any and all attempts to impose popular control not found elsewhere.

---

[8] In justice to the Bureau of Reclamation it should be said that in more than one instance the agriculturalists were largely responsible for initiating the reclamation projects now being criticized.

That the professional man should develop a measure of impatience or even contempt for the laity is natural. Many of the things which appear obvious to him must be explained step by step to the uninitiated. In consequence this ignorance seems simply appalling. Moreover, by virtue of his superior knowledge the professional man knows, or thinks he knows, what should be done in a given situation better than the uninformed public—or its political representatives. Thus professional educators insist that education is too important or too mysterious to be subject to the supervision of our politically elected municipal executives or even municipal legislatures. Instead, our educational systems must occupy an independent or quasi-independent status, one, incidentally, which professional educators will be able to dominate nine times out of ten. Similarly, our naval and military experts often confuse lay thinking by a barrage of technical detail in connection with the various projects up for consideration, and minimize within their departmental organization what they sometimes refer to as civilian interference but what is otherwise known as civilian control. It is true, of course, that all departments tend to develop departmental policies and attempt to "sell" these policies to the chief executive, the legislature, or the public as necessity may dictate. Nevertheless, there is a considerable difference between an endeavor "to sell a policy" to the public and an attempt "to jam it down the public's throat" with little or no regard for the fact that many of these departmental policies impinge upon matters over which the department in question has no jurisdiction, to which it has given little thought. In the opinion of a number of observers, at any rate, departmental integration on the basis of professional technique seems to accentuate the development of departmental arrogance in relation to the chief executive, the legislature, and to the general public as well.

Integration on this basis frequently leads to the appointment of narrow specialists as department heads. The result is frequently unfortunate both intra- and inter-departmentally. The appointment of a narrow specialist to the headship of a large administrative department may well result in departmental narrowness rather than in efficiency. Thus the appointment of a physicist to the head of a Department of Science may lead to an overemphasis of the mathematical sciences and the neglect of the organic sciences. Similarly the assignment of a chemical engineer to the management of a Department of Engineering might result in the neglect of the civil or hydraulic aspects of the department's work. Indeed, one of the reasons why state universities have insisted so vigorously upon a status more or less independent of the general educational system of the state has been the realization that professional schoolmen frequently dominate these educational systems and that under such auspices the state universities might be transformed into teachers' colleges to the neglect of their other activities.

The appointment of a specialist to the head of a department, it is urged, moreover, is likely to be conducive to promotions within the department upon the basis of technical efficiency rather than administrative ability. Technical ability is undoubtedly important; nevertheless, the management of a department calls for other and equally significant qualities—a breadth of vision and a capacity for leadership frequently not possessed by the mere technician.

The assignment of a specialist to the leadership of a department is very likely to accentuate the very difficulties of interdepartmental coördination that organization upon the basis of process itself precipitates. As has been indicated previously, a long career of specialization is very apt to produce loyalties to a particular profession, primary interest in the problems of that profession, and the neglect of most problems falling outside the bounds of that profession. Such a background, to put it mildly, scarcely tends to promote that interdepartmental understanding and sympathy which is imperative in the solution of interdepartmental problems.

The point can, perhaps, be stated more effectively another way. Breadth of knowledge, flexibility, and a capacity for administrative leadership are the prime requisites for a department head. This is so not only in the internal management of the departments but also in the conduct of its external relations. Only by the possession of these capacities can a department head properly administer his own department and maintain that relationship with other departments which is imperative if the administration of the government is to be maintained at a satisfactory level of efficiency. A lifetime of narrow specialization is not particularly conducive to an over-all vision. The fact that a man is an outstanding specialist in entomology has little or nothing to do with his capacity to coördinate the work of the Department of Agriculture, for example, with that of the Department of Public Works. His specialized knowledge relative to the habits and habitats of termites may contribute something to an understanding of wood construction and protection, but it will contribute little or nothing to an understanding of the problems connected with steel and concrete.

Moreover, the utilization of specialists drawn from the various professions as department heads will probably hamper the development of a system of interdepartmental transfer. Such a system is highly desirable if not imperative in the development of an over-all vision and that mutual understanding of the problems of the different departments which is necessary to the greatest degree of interdepartmental coordination and the utmost efficiency in the general adminis-tration.[9]

Finally, the development of these specialized departments with their emphasis upon means rather than ends will, so it is argued, have a disintegrating influence upon the chief executive's cabinet. Here more than anywhere breadth of view is imperative. The ends to which the energies of gov-ernment should be dedicated are paramount over the techni-cal procedures which should be followed in the attainment of those ends; but, in so far as the department exerts any influence upon its politically appointed head, it will be likely to emphasize the means rather than the ends. Stimuli for broad thinking relative to the purpose of government action will be lacking or appear only fortuitously.

CLIENTELE OR MATÉRIEL

A third possible method of departmental integration is upon the basis of clientele or matériel. This principle is, perhaps, best illustrated in the organization of the Veterans Administration "which deals with all the problems of the veterans, be they in health, in hospitals, in insurance, in wel-fare, or in education." The Immigration and Naturalization Service, the Children's Bureau, and the Office of Indian Affairs constitute still other illustrations. Each of these deals with its clientele in various relations. The Immigration and Naturalization Service handles the immigrant problem not from one side but from three—legal, financial, and medical. The Children's Bureau insists that just as the individual child cannot be divided into component parts but must in-stead remain a single entity, so its work must encompass

[9] It is pertinent to note in this connection that fourteen of the twenty permanent under secretaries heading administrative depart-ments in Great Britain in 1930 had received their appointment as the result of inter-departmental transfer.

all aspects of child welfare—health, education, and vocational guidance. The jurisdiction of the Office of Indian Affairs is even more sweeping, embracing practically all the governmental activities—health, educational, and financial—which relate to these wards of the nation. To some degree at least, it may be asserted that the Departments of Agriculture, Labor, and Commerce have been organized upon a similar pattern, in that they each serve the particular needs of some large segment of the body politic. In consequence, the Agricultural Extension Service, which from a functional point of view might well be placed under the Office of Education, is, in fact, part and parcel of the Department of Agriculture. For a long time the Federal Board for Vocational Education was attached to the Department of Labor. The Department of Commerce aspires to be the agency to which businessmen of the nation can come and feel certain of a friendly reception. The heads of these three departments look upon themselves more or less as spokesmen for their respective clienteles in the chief executive's cabinet. It should be noted, however, that the three departments are only partially organized upon this basis. In many particulars at least, their primary *raison d'être* is the solution of problems and the discharge of duties which fall in their respective fields.

Departmental integration on the basis of clientele has the great advantage of simplifying the relationship of the administration with the public. Veterans desirous of information relative to the various services which the government is prepared to render participants in the World War may ascertain the answer to any problem which may confront them directly from the Veterans Administration without being shunted from office to office. Similarly, the farmer interested in obtaining advice relative to any one of a number of problems which may arise in the conduct of his industry may do so at the Department of Agriculture. In this way the confusion and irritation so frequently attendant upon the public's transaction of business with the government is avoided.

Unquestionably the grouping of the subordinate administrative units into a departmental structure on the basis of clientele makes possible a coördination of the activities of the government with regard to particular segments of the public to a degree not attainable under any other form of organization.

The Office of Indian Affairs, for example, insists quite correctly that the Indians constitute a peculiar people who find it difficult if not impossible to adapt themselves to the demands of modern industrial civilization, that if they were left to themselves they would shortly be reduced to destitution, if not extinction. The Commissioner of Indian Affairs asserts consequently that it is the function of his office to protect the Indian in his existing status, and to effect, if possible, a gradual transformation of Indian habits and characteristics so that the Indian may at some future date take his place upon a plane of equality with his Caucasian contemporaries. This inevitably involves not only the temporary administration of Indian property but also instruction in at least the primary principles of personal and community hygiene, formal instruction in the schools, and vocational training in agriculture, the trades, and contemporary business practices.

Inevitably the question arises as to whether this task could not be more effectively accomplished if it were broken down into its component parts and the parts allocated to their various places in the administrative structure upon a functional basis. If this were done, the administration of Indian property would be turned over to one or other of the fiscal agencies of the government; the development of health standards to the United States Public Health Service; the educational activities to the Office of Education, and so on.

Such a proposal has more than once received serious consideration. But the answer both of the Indian administrators and of the leading students of Indian affairs has in each case been in the negative. In their opinion, the problems concerning the Indian tribes are so peculiarly related to Indian characteristics and so interrelated with each other that if they are to be solved at all they must be solved by a single agency. For these reasons it would be difficult to separate tutelage in personal hygiene from the formal instruction given in the schools; it would be no less difficult to separate the administration of Indian property from the endeavor both to effect a transformation in Indian character which will make the Indian self-sustaining, more or less sophisticated in the ways of a modern financial and industrial world, and at the same time to conserve enough tribal life to preserve the best of Indian culture.

On similar grounds, it is insisted that the multiplicity of problems which center in child life can better be solved as a single aggregation than treated individually. Hence the entire program of the federal government relative to prenatal care, child hygiene, preschool education, and the stimulation and enforcement of child-labor legislation has been concentrated in the hands of a single administrative unit.

The integration of all subordinate administrative units designed to serve certain segments of the body politic into a single department dedicated to the service of a given clientele, moreover, enables the department to consider the needs of its clientele from all angles, to work out a rounded treatment of their various problems, and so to coördinate the activities of these administrative units as to measurably increase their efficiency. To give a concrete illustration, the fact that the Bureau of Entomology and Plant Quarantine is in the same department with the Extension Service not only means that the farmers can secure the aid of a research organization in connection with plant diseases and insect pests, but that a vehicle exists for the transmission of this information to the interested public. Whether the vehicle would be equally effective if the Extension Service were under the auspices of the Office of Education is certainly controversial. As the Office of Education is now conceived it would probably be suicidal. Again, the fact that the Pure Food and Drug Administration was in the same department as the Bureau of Chemistry and Soils was, so it is asserted, conducive to a higher degree of coöperation between the two units than might otherwise have existed. When, for example, the Food and Drug Administration discovered that the use of Paris green as an insecticide resulted in the shipment of fruit to the market injurious to the public, chemists were immediately assigned to the task of discovering a substitute spray which could be used with a greater degree of safety. By virtue of this fact the needs of the Department's clientele were more effectively served than they might have been had these two units been in separate departments.

Another advantage of departmental organization according to clientele is the development of new skills in handling various complexes of problems, which frequently more than compensates for any loss of skill due either to lack of functionalization or to integration on a basis of process. Although the representative of the Children's Bureau may not have the medical training insisted upon by the Public Health Service or the educational background required by the Office of Education, she very shortly develops something the specialists rarely have, the capacity to size up an entire situation and to act accordingly. Moreover, in each case the representatives of these multifunctional agencies are sufficiently cognizant of the various aspects of their problem to know when to call in a specialist, if one is necessary.

No less important in terms of efficiency is the fact that under a great many circumstances the development of these multifunctional agencies on the basis of clientele or material avoids an excessive duplication both of personnel and of conflicting orders. Prior to the organization of the Department of Housing and Building Inspection in New York City, for instance, each tenement was subject to a separate "inspection at periodic intervals by men interested in slums, crime, fire escapes, plumbing, fire hazards, and electrical wiring." The inevitable result was not merely an excessive duplication of personnel, miles of unnecessary travel, an irritating duplication of intrusion into apartments but, surprisingly frequently, the issuance of conflicting orders relative to the steps to be taken to overcome alleged abuses. The integration of these various activities under the authority of a single agency has resulted both in a radical reduction in personnel and in the coördination of hitherto uncoördinated functions.

A striking advantage inherent in grouping the various and sundry bureaus into a departmental structure upon the basis of clientele may be the development of highly desirable administration–pressure-group relations. As an illustration, the relation of the Children's Bureau to the various women's clubs has given it support in the development of its programs and in its battles with the spoilsmen, and, equally important, has afforded it an exceedingly convenient vehicle for the dissemination of its educational program. The relation of the Department of Agriculture to the diverse agricultural pressure groups has gained for it at times the political support necessary for the development of

its program of service to the farmers and has similarly facilitated the work in agricultural education.

Over against these distinct advantages inherent in departmental integration on the basis of clientele or matériel have
been set a number of definite drawbacks.

In the first place, the principle is clearly incapable of
universal or even general application. Any such attempt
would lead to such a multiplicity of departments as to
frustrate the primary purpose of departmentalization—
coördination. As Viscount Haldane pointed out in his justly
famous *Report on the Machinery of Government,* a vigorous application of the principle would lead to a Department
of Youth, a Department of the Aged, a Department of Urban
Dwellers, a Department of Agriculture, a Department of
Manufacturers, a Department of Miners, a Department of
College Professors, a Department of Doctors, and so on.
The result would be such a multiplicity of small departments and administrations that the problem of interdepartmental coördination would be indistinguishable from that
which now exists at the bureau level.

Any such departmental pattern, moreover, would inevitably lead to jurisdictional conflict and duplication. Just what
should constitute the jurisdictional bounds, for example, of a
Department of the Aged? Would it undertake to furnish
those services which are the peculiar need of the aged—
(pensions, hospitalization, and the rest), or would it also
encompass within its jurisdiction water supply and fire protection? If it did the latter, the complexities of administration would become insurmountable.

If, on the other hand, the constituents of the Department
of the Aged are to be the recipients of services from a
Water Department, a Health Department, a Department of
Education, a Police Department, a Fire Department, *et al.,*

what becomes of the principle of integration on the basis of clientele? To say that the recipients of water, health, and educational services or of police and fire protection constitute the clientele of these several departments, is, of course, a mere juggling of words. Each and every individual in the entire community makes use of these several services. The plain truth is that the principle of integration on the basis of clientele possesses validity only when the congeries of problems which relate to a particular segment of the population are so evidently real and so closely interrelated that they can be solved effectively only if approached as a single complex rather than through the medium of their constituent elements.

Another inherent defect is the inevitable sacrifice of certain advantages of specialization. The fact that a single organization combines within its compass diverse functions makes this inescapable. Thus the head of the Veterans Administration "must supervise and direct specialists in administration, insurance, vocational education, and rehabilitation." The chief of the Children's Bureau must direct specialists in health, education, and labor. Tenement house inspectors must undertake to pass judgment upon plumbing, wiring, living conditions, and fire hazards. Obviously, no one man can know as much about each of these as could a group composed of specialists in each field. This criticism, it should be admitted, however, is likewise applicable in more or less degree to departments organized both upon the basis of function and work processes.

Also significant from the point of view of administrative efficiency is the fact that departments organized upon the basis of clientele or matériel, in contrast to those based upon work processes, rarely provide a sufficient volume of work of a given sort to make possible a completely satisfactory division of labor, or, equally important, to provide satisfactory careers upon the basis of which capable persons will be attracted into the government service.

Finally, under certain circumstances at least, this pattern of departmental integration is said to render administration unduly subservient to the demands of the pressure groups. The Veterans Administration is generally conceded to be very sympathetic to the Veterans' Lobby, throwing the weight of its influence behind the demands of King Legion in season and out. It is likewise charged that the Departments of Agriculture, Labor, and Commerce are all unnecessarily responsive at times to the demands of organized interests as against general public interests in their respective fields.

TERRITORY

A fourth method of departmental organization is that based upon place or territory. This technique has long been used as a basis of intradepartmental organization both in the national government and in the state and local areas. In the Department of State, for example, there is a Division of Western European Affairs, of Eastern European Affairs, of Far Eastern Affairs, of Near Eastern Affairs, of Mexican Affairs, of Latin American Affairs, and so on. In many of the larger cities, the police department is divided into precincts; almost complete supervisory authority is delegated to the precinct captain through whom all communications both from and to headquarters must go. A similar situation is frequently found in connection with the construction and maintenance of streets, sewers, and various public works.

This technique has been applied at the departmental level principally in connection with overseas possessions. In Great Britain the Indian administration is placed in the India Office, matters affecting Dominion relations in the Dominion Office, and the management of the Crown colonies in the

Colonial Office. In Japan, the Ministry for Overseas Affairs looks after colonial matters. A Ministry for Italian Africa handles African problems for Fascist Italy.

In the United States, the Bureau of Insular Affairs and the Division of Territories, formerly in the Departments of Navy and Interior, respectively, represent similar developments. But the relative insignificance of our overseas empire, together with the fact that the larger proportion of that empire is in such close proximity to the United States as to be practically a part of our continental domain, makes any immediate application of the principle upon a departmental scale inexpedient.

Departmentalization upon the basis of place or territory has not been wholly confined to administrative units dealing with overseas possessions, however. This is evidenced not only by the continued existence of a Secretary of State for Scotland in Great Britain, but—radically different though it is—by the recent creation of the Tennessee Valley Authority and the further proposal to create seven additional regions similar in character centering around the great river valleys of the United States.

To some extent departmental integration upon this basis partakes of the nature of the geographic decentralization discussed previously. The two concepts, however, are distinct and separate. The governmental decentralization, analyzed earlier, generally involves not merely the delegation of administrative power but legislative and political authority as well. Once these powers have been delegated, they can usually be abrogated only by legislative, or under certain circumstances, constitutional action. By contrast, departmentalization on the basis of place or territory is concerned only with the organization and distribution of administrative power. And, under all circumstances, the Chief Executive will legally continue to exercise the same degree of control over the subordinate administrative units, grouped in such a department, as he would had they been grouped together upon any other basis.

The advantages of departmental integration on the basis of place or territory are most apparent in connection with overseas possessions. The great distances which separate colonial possessions from the seat of government and the relatively greater difficulties of communication make the maintenance of direct lines of authority from the field services to functional or process departments and the clearing of interdepartmental difficulties through the home office a slow and cumbersome process. To use a British illustration, insistence upon direct communication between the health and educational services of India with the Ministries of Health and Education, respectively, and upon ironing out interdepartmental differences between those services through the medium of officials resident in London would be patently absurd. In the first place, it would necessitate the intervention of two or three men in the departmental hierarchy at home who would in all probability know less about the situation in India than the men in the field; second, it would lead to interminable delays; and, third, it would clutter up the home ministries with matters largely alien to their major interests.[10] Under these circumstances, consequently, it should be apparent that effective administration demands the grouping of subordinate administrative units in India under some sort of central supervisory authority. Whether this should be considered a departmental division of the Imperial Government or a separate

[10] It should be conceded that recognition by the British that the ultimate status of India must be dominion status has also contributed to the geographic decentralization which characterizes Indian administration. In other words, political as well as administrative considerations enter the picture.

and independent government is largely a matter of nomenclature. In any event, such a grant of supervisory authority to officials in India would necessitate the organization of a home office or department possessing a commensurate breadth of supervisory power. The principal concern of the home office will be not the supervision of the day-to-day detail of the Indian Service, but the coördination of the larger aspects of colonial administration with the policies of the home government.

This departmental pattern in the government of overseas possessions, moreover, facilitates the adaptation of administrative policies and regulations to the needs of the area over which the department has jurisdiction. This is so not merely because a greater degree of discretion is delegated to administrative officials on the ground than is customary under any other mode of organization, but also because a more effective mechanism is provided through which the needs of the local area can be represented at the general headquarters. Thus not only has the Indian Service been given a relatively free hand in working out the solutions of problems of health and education in India in the light of Indian conditions, as a result of which the many facets of these problems have been called to the attention of the Service much more forcibly than would have been the case if the ultimate decision had been made in England; but no less important has been the fact that the entire administration of India heads up in a single agency —the India Office. Because of this, the peculiar needs and demands of India have probably received much more attention than they would have if these had been isolated incidents in the administration of some twenty different departments. Convergence upon a single department has given them such force and volume that they could hardly be overlooked.

Owing to the relative insignificance of our overseas empire and the proximity of much of what there is to continental United States, this principle of departmentalization has made little or no progress here. Curiously enough, however, the United States furnishes one of the two outstanding examples of the principle in connection with the internal administration of a modern country: the first is, of course, the Secretary of State for Scotland; second, the Tennessee Valley Administration.

The infrequent utilization of the principle in internal administrative organization in contrast to its general use in connection with overseas possessions inevitably raises a question as to its applicability to internal affairs. It is certainly hard to believe that the burden of administration in the smaller countries of the world—Switzerland, Sweden—will ever become such as to render decentralization in this fashion imperative. In countries possessing vast stretches of territory, however, the factor of distance may be just as complicating administratively as it is in connection with the administration of an overseas empire. The problem may, of course, be solved through some form of federalism. Nevertheless, as we have already discovered, federalism has the tremendous disadvantage of failing to provide a mechanism of coördination adequate to the exigencies of a complicated national economy. Under these circumstances, consequently, it may well be that departmentalization upon the basis of place or territory may be that exact compromise between the advantages of decentralization and centralization which is thought desirable.

To state the case for the domestic application of this technique of departmentalization necessitates a repetition of much that has been said previously. The desirability of a rounded analysis alone justifies the redundancy.

As has already been implied in our previous discussions,

departmental integration upon this basis permits a greater coördination of the services rendered and control exercised within a given area than would otherwise be possible. Thus the concentration of the development of the Tennessee River Valley in the hands of a single federal agency has made possible an integration of the various engineering, power, navigation, housing, and agricultural projects which would have been unattainable under any other form of organization.

Internally as well as externally this pattern facilitates the special adaptation of governmental policies to the needs of the areas affected. Thus the tremendous power resources of the Tennessee Valley have impelled the T.V.A. to concentrate upon the construction of dams and the development of electrical energy. Elsewhere the emphasis might have been quite different.

No less important than either of the preceding advantages is the fact that this mode of departmentalization also furnishes an effective medium through which the needs and aspirations of the people of the different sections can be presented to the administration. This is true not only of the day-to-day detail of administration which can be influenced by the direct impacts of local residents upon the departmental managers, but also in connection with these larger aspects of public policy in which the regions have a distinctly sectional point of view. The mechanism will, of course, be all the more effective if the heads of these regional departments are natives of the regions over which they preside. Thus the existence of a Secretary of State for Scotland has undoubtedly created the feeling and perhaps the actuality that the peculiar needs of this northern non-English section of the British Isles are being more effectively looked after than would otherwise be the case. The substitution of a single agency of government operating over a large area for ten or twelve functional departments, moreover, should simplify intergovernmental relations. Thus a single regional department of the federal government covering New England or the Old South should not only simplify the working out of intergovernmental agreements, but should also minimize those interdepartmental conflicts which inevitably contribute to intergovernmental confusion and irritation under a federal form of government.

Incidentally, this form of departmental organization, so it is asserted, should result in numerous economies of operation, even in a country like the United States. Although the distance from New York to Seattle is not as great as that from London to Calcutta, it is nevertheless of significant proportions. The delegation of broad supervisory authority to administrative officers located on the West coast should consequently cut radically both travel and communication costs, minimize paper work, and permit the more effective disposition of the regional personnel.[11]

If, however, the application of this principle of departmentalization domestically possesses distinct advantages, it also has inherent in it certain serious drawbacks. In the first place, it should be obvious that it inevitably increases the difficulties in the way of developing and administering uniform national policies. Although the maintenance of uniform policies is by no means universally desirable, nevertheless, there are certain fields in which they are imperative. There is, for example, a minimum below which the administration of the health laws of the nation cannot be allowed to fall.

Similarly, if the military defenses of the country are to

[11] It should be conceded, however, that many of these advantages could be attained (1) by regionalizing the field staff of each functional department, (2) by granting this staff proper discretion, and (3) by developing a mechanism of regional contacts between the small agencies.

be maintained in a reasonable state of efficiency it is apparent that there must not only be uniformity of drill and equipment, but unity of command as well. If the navy is to be of any significance in the defense of either our continental or overseas empire, it must operate as a unit and not as a series of disjointed segments. In so far, consequently, as this mode of departmentalization undermines the unity of administration in those spheres in which unity is imperative, it *ipso facto* impairs its own *raison d'être*.

Although the maintenance of military and naval departments upon a regional basis might be feasible in time of peace, it is quite evident that in time of war, when the whole power of the nation must be concentrated upon single points of attack or defense, such an organizational pattern would be catastrophic. The time which would be lost in negotiating interregional agreements might easily suffice to lose a war. Only the power of supreme command organized along functional lines is adequate to meet the potentialities of such a situation. Again, it must be remarked, the time element in the military sphere is highly critical. In the civilian sphere, with rare exceptions, such is not the case. Nevertheless, even here diverse interpretations of national statutes and strictness or laxness in law enforcement might easily lead to the overthrow of national standards. Failure to enforce the Pure Food and Drug Law in one section of the country, for example, would not merely have an injurious effect upon that region, but upon all regions into which the food, produced or processed, was shipped. Similarly, the strict enforcement of the National Labor Relations Act in one section of the country but lax enforcement in another could place the entrepreneurs of the former region at a disadvantage in the market with those of the latter. The segmentation of the administration of the trust policy might lead to the acquiescence in monopoly in one section of the country at the very time aggressive action against trusts was being taken in another.

It is to be assumed, of course, that some over-all agency centering in the national executive would to a large extent counteract these tendencies. Nevertheless, the burden of centralization and coördination which would thus be imposed upon the chief executive would be infinitely greater than it is today. Whether the gains which might be attained through this method of departmentalization would offset the difficulties involved is certainly controversial. Departmental integration on the basis of place or territory possesses, in other words, many of the defects inherent in governmental decentralization along federal lines. Their gravity is in direct ratio to the necessity for the maintenance of a uniform system of law and policy throughout the nation.

These objections, be it said parenthetically, are less cogently applicable to an overseas colonial empire than they are to an integral part of a homogeneous territory. Not only do varying geographic, economic, social, and even racial characteristics of many colonial empires justify great diversity in governmental policy, but the element of distance, in and of itself, acts as a protection. Acquiescence in submarginal health standards along the east coast of, Africa, for instance, in no way jeopardizes the health of the entire British Empire. Similarly, an inadequate educational system in French Indo-China in no way impairs the industrial efficiency of European France. Moreover, the imperial defense forces are usually, if not universally, under the control of the mother country.

A further disadvantage inherent in departmentalization upon the basis of place or territory is that it may well be conducive to an overemphasis upon regional in contrast to national thinking.

One of the great differences between the executive and the legislative departments of the government of the United States as they are now organized is that the former is inclined to think in national terms, the latter in terms of their respective states or constituencies. At times, e.g., the period from 1861 to 1865, it has been the executive which has held the country together. Departmental integration on the basis of place or territory would, it is charged, radically weaken the centrifugal influence of the executive and greatly enhance the tendency toward sectionalism, both economic and political. And in so doing it might easily lead to disturbing consequences. In any event, a reduction in national thinking is not an end to be desired, for, with the increasing integration of our economic life, more and more of our problems are becoming national, fewer and fewer regional in character.

Less potentially catastrophic, but nevertheless not without significance, is the fact that the introduction of the principle of territorial departmentalization on a general scale might well prevent the development of that degree of specialization which is imperative to the attainment of a maximum of efficiency in the conduct of administration, at least in certain lines. This might well be true if for no other reason than that the division of the country into a series of geographic areas would automatically reduce the volume of work under each of the departments. Thus the Bureau of Agricultural Engineering and Public Roads and the Corps of Engineers which, by virtue of the volume of work they handle, scattered, as it is, over the entire country, have succeeded in building up and maintaining an efficient corps of engineers, might no longer be able to do so. Whether there would be a sufficient volume of engineering work in each of the twelve or fifteen regional departments into which the country might be divided to make possible the specialization or provide the opportunities for a governmental career in engineering is a question as yet unanswered. And needless to say, the problem would not be confined to the engineering services. Instead, it would encompass all the technical services now centered in Washington.

The mere matter of drawing the geographic boundaries of these regional departments would itself be a difficult and complex task. A survey of administrative decentralization as it now exists within the functional and process departments reveals almost as many distinct administrative areas as there are departments. The Department of War, for example, is organized into nine army corps; the Federal Reserve Board into twelve Federal Reserve Districts; the Rural Electrification Administration centers everything in Washington and operates directly from the national capital; by contrast, the Department of Agriculture utilizes each of the forty-eight states. Even where two or more departments use the same geographic area, experience has often dictated the utilization of different foci. Thus while a number of federal agencies operating in Michigan have located their headquarters in Detroit, an equal number whose work necessitates close coöperation with the state government have centered their activities in Lansing. In short, there are no "natural boundaries" for administrative devolution which encompass at one and the same time all the administrative activities of the federal government. Instead, the boundaries vary according to the nature of the work being carried on. Any attempt to delineate such boundaries, therefore, would not only encounter a multiplicity of difficulties, but might indeed necessitate the sacrifice of so many advantages inherent in other departmental patterns as to much more than offset any possible gains.

Still another result of the grouping of the various subordinate administrative units into regional departments might be a serious diminution of the prestige of the national service. Curiously enough, the Biblical aphorism, a prophet is not without honor save in his own country, seems to be as true in contemporary administration as it was in Galilee. To a surprising degree the primary function of the national administration, particularly in the very important ever-expanding sphere of federal-state relationship, is that of furnishing instruction and leadership to the state services. Although the effectiveness of the leadership furnished rests in part upon the personality and capacity of the federal agents, it also depends, to a surprising degree, upon the prestige of the federal service. This in turn rests partly upon the superior training required for entrance into the federal administration, partly upon the breadth of experience gained in that service, and partly upon the respect engendered by emissaries from the seat of the national government. Departmentalization upon the basis of place or territory would to some degree at least nullify these advantages. In the first place, organization on such a basis would in all probability reduce the breadth of experience these federal agents now obtain. In the second place, it would certainly diminish, if it did not eliminate, the element of prestige which accrues to the individual agent by virtue of his alleged relationship with the seat of power. The total result of this might be a serious diminution of those psychological factors which today enable the federal departments to furnish relatively effective leadership to both state and municipal administrations.

No less important than any of the foregoing is the fact that this form of departmental organization might also lead to the domination of these regional departments by local politicians and local pressure groups.

The American party system has been defined as a "federation of local machines held together by the co-hesive power of public plunder." The definition is obvi-ously unfair and inaccurate, nevertheless it illustrates a point. The party organization in the United States is pre-dominantly state or regional in character, so much so, that despite the theoretically national character of our admin-istrative organization, the statutes themselves provide that assignments to·the civil service shall be proportionate to the population of the various states. Nor does the regional pressure stop here. The system of senatorial courtesy en-ables the senators, particularly if they are from the major-ity party, to dictate appointments to many offices not embraced by the civil service laws. If, then, this situa-tion exists in the face of an allegedly nationalistic form of departmentalization, what would take place if the depart-ments were organized on an avowedly regional basis? The existing pressure, which to some extent is held in check by the national character of the administrative organiza-tion and which to a considerable degree operates *sub rosa,* would in all probability boldly come out into the open. The time-honored tradition of "self-determination" and "home rule" would shortly be marshaled to justify the complete dominance of the national administration by the local politicians, with the result that both the efficiency and integrity of the national administration might easily be impaired.

Closely allied to, and indeed an inseparable part of, the demands of the local politicians would be the efforts of the local pressure groups. Needless to say, pressure-group activities are not necessarily pernicious. In a sense, the Constitution of the United States may be said to have been the work of pressure groups. In like fashion, our tariff policy has been the resultant of pressure-group activities. The Civil Service Reform League can claim at least partial credit for the adoption of the merit system. But in each of these cases the policy finally adopted has been the result of the play of forces in the national arena. To some extent at least, selfish local interests have canceled each other or have led to beneficial compromises. No such corrective would exist if the administration were departmentalized along regional lines. Instead, The Associated Manufacturers of New England might conceivably dominate the administration of the Department of New England, with the result that in New England the enforcement of the national labor law might easily become difficult if not impossible. Similarly, the "Cotton Growers Association" might dictate the broad lines of the enforcement in the Department of Southern Affairs, thereby frustrating all efforts to alleviate the condition of the tenant farmers. The simple fact is that vested interests of this character occasionally become more or less dominant even in the nationally organized departments. It seems highly probable, consequently, that their influence would be even more radical in departments organized upon a regional rather than a national basis.

So serious are these defects that except for the recent suggestion that the seven great river valleys of the United States be so organized, one might be inclined to dismiss quite categorically the concept of departmentalization upon the basis of place or territory.

Indeed, if the preceding analysis has revealed anything, it is that the study of administration has not as yet developed a set of scientific principles relative to the problem of departmental integration capable of precise application.

Instead, it is evident that the concepts we have been discussing are at best a series of generalizations deduced from past experience. Down to date the exact nature of these concepts has not been carefully defined, nor have their boundaries been accurately delineated. Moreover, the advantages which each of these several modes of organization is sometimes said to possess are, under certain circumstances at least, offset by a multiplicity of weaknesses. To a very considerable extent the utilization of one of these modes of departmental organization rather than another turns upon the objective sought. If, as we have previously indicated, the paramount purpose of a departmental structure is action—the solution of a given problem or congeries of problems—then organization upon the basis of function may be most desirable. If, on the other hand, as in the case of a Department of Engineering, the primary purpose is the economies and efficiencies which may. be achieved in the operations of professional staffs or the use of expensive machinery, the proper basis of departmentalization may be work processes. Under some circumstances the necessities or convenience of certain segments of the population may seem more important than mere mechanical efficiency—whether that efficiency be achieved by coordination according to function or according to work processes. Under other circumstances it may be desirable to attain a considerable measure of governmental decentralization without resorting to the expedient of federalism. In such situations departmentalization upon the basis of place or territory may offer a satisfactory solution. Thus it is evident that the controlling factor in determining the foundation upon which a departmental structure should rest is not some abstract concept of administration but the paramount objective to which the department is dedicated. Equally obvious is it, however, that the mere application of one of these concepts will not *ipso facto* produce the desired grouping. Instead, the advantages and disadvantages of each of these modes of departmental integration must be weighed in connection with each addition to the departmental structure. And as past experience and present practice clearly indicate, the result will be a departmental organization in which one or at the most two of these concepts of departmentalization will predominate, but in which all four methods of integration will play a significant role.

The mere fact that these several concepts have not as yet attained the precision of a scientific formula does not, however, render them valueless. Far from it, for vaguely defined and poorly delineated as they are, subject to all the qualifications, limitations, and exceptions that have been noted in the preceding pages, they constitute nevertheless an exceedingly useful frame of reference for further thinking upon the subject.

VI ◆ ◆

ADMINISTRATIVE REGULATION AND
THE INDEPENDENT REGULATORY AGENCIES

AN INTEGRAL PART OF THE PROBLEM OF GROUPING SUB-
ordinate administrative units into a departmental structure, but nevertheless distinct from it, is the question of
the proper situs of the independent regulatory agencies in
the administrative organization. Beginning with the creation of the Interstate Commerce Commission in 1887, these
units have expanded and multiplied until today they are ten
in number. Of these, the Federal Communications Commission, the Federal Power Commission, the Federal Trade
Commission, the Interstate Commerce Commission, the National Labor Relations Board and the Securities Exchange
Commission are, of course, outstanding. Merely to list them
is to indicate how vast is the segment of administration now
being carried on outside the departmental structure. And if
the reasoning upon which these have been based is to be
adhered to in the future, the existing situation is but a prelude to a further development of the federal administration
which, if carried to extremes, may lead to serious consequences.

The reasoning which has justified the creation of these
agencies may be epitomized as follows. In the first place,
many of them exercise judicial or quasi-judicial authority.
This fact alone, in the opinion of many members of Congress, was sufficient reason for assigning them a status in
the administration independent of the departmental organ-

ization, for in the very nature of things it seemed desirable to protect the exercise of this function against both political and administrative pressure. Such protection, in the opinion of these representatives, could not be assured within the traditional departmental organization. The great administrative departments have for the most part been headed by politically appointed Secretaries, Assistant Secretaries and administrative assistants many of whom have been much more interested in the political repercussions of the activities under their supervision than they have been in the activities themselves. In view of these circumstances it was highly probable that these departmental officers might, on occasion at least, interfere with the regulatory agencies even in the exercise of their judicial functions. It seemed wise, consequently, to take note of this potentiality and to provide against it. As a result there developed a general tendency to give the principal regulatory agencies engaged in exercising judicial authority a position outside of the departmental structure.

The fact that many of these agencies also exercised legislative authority undoubtedly accentuated the development of this administrative pattern. Although this was probably not as decisive in the legislative mind as the care for judicial independence, it did suggest a relationship between these agencies and Congress different from that which characterized the routine administrative subdivisions. Quasi-legislative power, it is true, has been conferred upon certain administrative units in certain departments, but there always existed the possibility that it might be employed by politically minded departmental officers to serve partisan, or even personal, ends—a possibility which recurring scandals in some departments painfully illustrated. By such experiences, the feeling that peculiar safeguards should be thrown around continuing grants of broad discretionary authority was increased rather than diminished.

In addition, the legislature evidently believed that, under certain conditions at least, rule-making could more safely be entrusted to an independent board than to a single official or departmental committee, and upon one occasion even went so far as to provide for regional representation. In taking this position Congress was of course projecting into the administrative field the reasoning which justifies the existing organization of representative assemblies for purposes of policy determination.

In other instances, Congress quite obviously looked upon the work of these independent agencies as highly exploratory in character, designed to furnish it with a basis for definitive legislative action later, rather than to discharge mere routine duties in administration. In some respects the units in question appeared to be more nearly analogous to legislative investigating committees than they did to mere administrative subdivisions. In any event, the result of these various considerations was to strengthen the tendency to grant regulatory bodies an independent status in the administration rather than to subordinate them to departmental supervision and control.

Similarly contributing to the rise of this "fourth" branch of the government was the prestige which accrued to the Interstate Commerce Commission as a result of its apparent success in handling difficult problems. And, finally, in many cases there simply was no suitable department to which the proposed agencies might be assigned.

Despite the apparent soundness of the reasoning which underlay the creation of these agencies, recent decades have witnessed a growing volume of criticism aimed at both their independent status and their organization. This criticism has, for the most part, emanated from two major sources: from the exponents of the doctrine of executive management and from those who believe in a greater degree of judicial control.

The point of view represented by the first school of thought is best summarized in the Report of the President's Committee on Administrative Management. The mere existence of the independent regulatory agencies, in the opinion of the authors of that Report, interferes with, and to a considerable extent renders impossible, both over-all planning and, no less important, the coördination of the execution of such public policies as may be adopted. Because of this fact, these agencies, in the opinion of these experts, not only impair the constitutional mandate imposed upon the chief executive to recommend to the consideration of Congress "such measures as he may judge necessary and expedient" but they also interfere with those broader responsibilities which have been imposed upon him by virtue of his position as party leader. Thus, time and again, they point out, these independent authorities have enunciated plans relative to the specific segments of the economy over which they have jurisdiction completely at variance with those which have been formulated by the chief executive himself. The result has been that, contrary to the intention of the Founding Fathers and the necessities of party government, leadership in the formulation of public policy has been diffused rather than coördinated.

In addition, it is argued under the head of administrative management that as long as these agencies maintain their independence there is always the possibility, and occasionally the actuality, that they may exercise their discretion in such a way as to stultify the broader policies of the Administration. For example, a vigorous "trust-busting"

President may find himself seriously handicapped by the lethargy of a cartel-minded Federal Trade Commission; or, conversely, a cartel-minded chief executive may find himself frustrated by the "trust-busting" activities of this same commission. Thus not only may the work of the several segments of the administration fail to mesh, but they may even be dedicated to diverse purposes. The Humphrey case, it will be recalled, arose in large measure out of just such a situation.

Also disintegrating in influence, from the standpoint of the proponents of executive management, is the effect which the independence of these regulatory agencies may soon have upon the orderly processes of administration *per se*. Not only does their status give rise to jurisdictional conflicts which can only be settled by appeal to Congress, but their insistence upon complete self-sufficiency frequently leads to an unnecessary expansion of their legal, economic, and statistical services.

Pertinent to this line of argument is the obvious fact that the increasing utilization of these independent boards and commissions is leading to irresponsible government. Theoretically responsible to Congress, they are, in fact, responsible to no one. Congress has neither the time, inclination, nor the machinery to maintain effective supervision over them. Nor has it ever made a serious effort to do so. The result has been that, save for the presentation of an annual report to Congress, or an occasional investigation, these agencies have been monarchs of their respective domains, efficient or inefficient in the prosecution of their duties as the consciences and capacities of the individual commissioners may dictate. In this they stand in striking contrast to most administrators within the departmental structure whose activities are at all times subject to the scrutiny of a department head appointed by the President of the United States; he in turn is elected or rejected by the people of the United States every four years.

With considerable cogency, the exponents of the doctrine of executive management maintain that the very organization of these regulatory agencies as it exists at the present time impairs the impartial handling of the most important phase of their work. Not only is the same body law maker and administrator; often it is also prosecutor and judge. Such a concentration of power, it is true, frequently exists at the extremities of the administrative process, as for example, when a policeman interprets the law prior to making an arrest; nevertheless the analogy is not foursquare. The policeman's action is reviewed both as to fact and to law, not only by a desk sergeant but also by a prosecutor's office and an impartial judge—the actions of all of these are subject to still further review on appeal by higher courts. By contrast, so it is charged, these so-called quasi-judicial agencies combine in one body the direction and control of the policeman, the prosecutor and the judge. Their decisions, moreover, can frequently be appealed only on questions of law and not of fact.

Convinced of the validity of their criticism, the proponents of the doctrine of executive management insist that a radical alteration in the organization and status of these regulatory bodies is imperative. The alternative to this radical alteration, as they see it, is to witness the transformation of the federal administration into a "grotesque agglomeration of independent and irresponsible units, bogged by the weight and confusion of the whole crazy structure." [1] Such a development can only be averted, they declare, by integrating these agencies in the departmental structure on the terms set forth in the Report of the President's Com-

[1] *Report of the President's Committee on Administrative Management* (Washington, 1937), p. 41.

mittee on Administrative Management, the essence of which
is contained in the paragraphs which follow:

Under this proposed plan the regulatory agency would be set
up, not in a governmental vacuum outside the executive department, but within a department. There it would be divided into an
administrative section and a judicial section. The administrative
section would be a regular bureau or division in the department,
headed by a chief with career tenure and staffed under civil-
service regulations. It would be directly responsible to the Secretary and through him to the President. The judicial section, on
the other hand, would be "in" the department only for purposes
of "administrative housekeeping," such as the budget, general
personnel administration, and matériel. It would be wholly independent of the department and the President with respect to its
work and its decisions. Its members would be appointed by the
President with the approval of the Senate for long, staggered
terms and would be removable only for causes stated in the
statute.

The division of work between the two sections would be relatively simple. The first procedural steps in the regulatory process
as now carried on by the independent commissions would go to
the administrative section. It would formulate rules, initiate
action, investigate complaints, hold preliminary hearings, and by
a process of sifting and selection prepare the formal record of
cases which is now prepared in practice by the staffs of the commissions. It would, of course, do all the purely administrative or
sublegislative work now done by the commissions—in short all
the work which is not essentially judicial in nature. The judicial
section would sit as an impartial, independent body to make
decisions affecting the public interest and private rights upon the
basis of the records and findings presented to it by the administrative section. In certain types of cases where the volume of
business is large and quick and routine action is necessary, the
administrative section itself should in the first instance decide
the cases and issue orders, and the judicial section should sit as
an appellate body to which such decisions could be appealed on
questions of law.[2]

[2] *Ibid.*, p. 41.

In this fashion, the proponents of the plan insist, it would be possible to safeguard the judicial work of the independent regulatory agencies and at the same time to minimize the defects inherent in the present mode of organization. The integration of the administrative and quasi-legislative aspects of the activities of the commissions into the departmental structure should not only minimize the present interference with over-all planning, but, no less important, it should make possible a relatively complete degree of policy co-ordination. It should, furthermore, accelerate the settlement of jurisdictional disputes and retard the present trend toward unnecessary duplication. In addition, the separation of the administrative and policy-determining functions of these commissions from the judicial should make for an increased specialization which in turn should be reflected in increased efficiency in both types of work. And, as a crowning advantage, it should eliminate a much criticized feature of the existing procedure—the practice of combining the office of prosecutor and judge in a single agency.

Although the members of the President's Committee nowhere go into the problem of administrative regulation in all its ramifications, they have, by implication at least, set the seal of their approval upon the existing organization and procedure of the regulatory units which are now incorporated in the departmental structure—at least in so far as their subordination to the chief executive is concerned. They are, in other words, thoroughgoing exponents of the doctrine of executive management.

The proposal of the President's Committee on Administrative Management has everywhere been received with respect; it has also encountered vigorous criticism.

In a recent volume entitled *Federal Regulatory Action and Control,* F. F. Blachly and M. E. Oatman conclude an elaborate analysis of the present system with the following words:

> The organization and the operations of the administrative agencies, particularly those agencies which perform functions affecting individual rights, are carefully devised to combine the protection of guaranteed rights with the promotion of administrative efficiency. The constitutional and statutory basis of administration, the forms of administrative action, the enforcement methods and controls applicable to the respective forms, and the special devices for obtaining efficiency contribute to both these ends. The system is not perfect, but it is constantly being improved as to efficiency, at the same time that its operations are devised and controlled in such a way that guaranteed rights are safeguarded.[3]

With this as their fundamental postulate, the authors then turn to a critique of the proposal of the President's Committee. Their analysis is largely technical and follows the pattern set by the major modes of action of the regulatory bodies themselves.

The first series of questions to which these authors address themselves is whether: (1) the issuance of rules and regulations of the type now formulated by the regulatory agencies should be handled by a board or by a single individual; (2) whether they are of such a nature that they should emanate from a single agency; and (3) whether such action should be subjected to any particular control.

In so far as procedural rules and regulations are concerned, the authors conclude that the burden of proof lies on those who propose to change the existing situation, and that down to date no adequate proof that a radical change is

---

[3] *Federal Regulatory Action and Control,* F. F. Blachly and M. E. Oatman (Washington, 1940), p. 140. The author wishes at this point to acknowledge his deep indebtedness to F. F. Blachly and M. E. Oatman upon whose analysis he has leaned heavily at several points in this chapter.

necessary has been furnished. In a somewhat different category, in their opinion, are those rules and regulations which are substantive in character. These are essentially legislative in their nature. In consequence, the same arguments can be advanced in behalf of their formulation by a collegial body as are used to justify representative government itself. No problem of separation of powers arises in this connection since the function is purely legislative and not judicial in its nature. For the same reason the problem of keeping "these rules and regulations in line with Congressional policy and holding them within the general limits of law" is essentially a legislative and judicial, and not an executive responsibility.

But what of the second category of activities in which these independent regulatory agencies engage, to wit, investigation? "It is clearly inappropriate," in the opinion of these authors, "for the Executive to control investigation generally." Some investigations are carried on for the information of the legislature; others are made upon the complaint of some one who deems himself injured by an unlawful action; still others are instituted by the regulatory authority itself. In all three cases they are usually a preliminary to legislative or judicial action. Hence nothing could be gained and much might be lost by subjecting these agencies to administrative control.

The third general category into which the activities of these independent regulatory agencies fall is that of the prosecution of cases. In this connection Blachly and Oatman emphasize the fact that such activity is limited to a relatively narrow segment of the commissions' work. The question of prosecution, they point out, arises, or appears to arise, chiefly in respect to: (1) reparation orders; (2) injunction and command orders; and (3) certain orders suspending or revoking licenses because of violations of laws or rules and regulations. Reparation orders, the authors contend, are essentially acts of adjudication. Accordingly the question of separating the prosecuting from the judicial function is irrelevant. Such is not the case, however, with those orders which are customarily referred to as injunctive or command. Nevertheless, even here it should be noted that in practically every instance "where prosecution and adjudication are performed by the same agency, they are not performed by the same individual" [4] and that in all cases "review of the cease and desist order can be had in the circuit court of appeals—a guaranty against arbitrary, willful or biased action by the Commission." [5]

Although there would appear to be a similar mixture of functions in connection with orders suspending or revoking licenses, no evidence has so far been adduced of undesirable consequences resulting from the present procedure. Until such evidence is advanced, it would hardly be the course of wisdom to abandon that procedure for purely theoretical reasons.

The principal means by which the several regulatory boards and commissions take action is, of course, through the medium of statutory orders. Again the vital question must be asked: What advantage would be gained by separating the administrative and legislative from the judicial sections of these agencies in connection with the issuance of these orders? Many of these orders are essentially legislative in their character, and for this reason, in the opinion of the authors, should be issued by collegial bodies directly responsible to Congress and not by a single administrator responsible to the chief executive. But even in connection with orders which are essentially judicial in their character, there appears to be no evidence which *ipso facto* makes a

[4] *Ibid.*, p. 157.
[5] *Ibid.*, p. 157.

separation of the administrative and judicial functions imperative. In large measure these orders fall into five categories: (1) injunction and command; (2) reparation or analogous orders; (3) penalty orders; (4) orders in respect to licenses, privileges, grants, permits and the like; and (5) negative orders. Without attempting to epitomize their line of reasoning further, suffice it to say that Blachly and Oatman concede a situation which needs correction only in the case of one particular category of injunction and command orders, i.e., the cease and desist orders of the Federal Trade Commission.

The upshot of this analysis is that, in the opinion of the authors, the independent boards and commissions do not constitute "a haphazard deposit of irresponsible agencies and uncoördinated power." Quite the contrary, they are performing the work which has been assigned to them with a relatively high degree of efficiency.

Dissent from the proposal put forward by the President's Committee on Administrative Management, however, does not rest exclusively upon the technical reasoning advanced by Blachly and Oatman. Equally vigorous is the dissent which rests upon reasons of broad public policy.

The proposal to integrate the independent agencies into the departmental structure would, these latter writers insist, result in the concentration of too much power in the hands of a single individual—a power which might be used for personal or partisan purposes just as readily as for purposes purely administrative. That Presidents of the United States have used the great authority of their office for partisan purposes is a fact which hardly needs to be labored Only rarely, it is true, has this pressure been directed against the regulatory processes now under departmental control. Nevertheless, even here they have undoubtedly given "tone" to the administration. Some strong executives of the United States—Jefferson, Jackson, Lincoln, Cleveland, Theodore Roosevelt, Wilson, and Franklin Roosevelt—have represented particular combinations of interests, sectional, class or economic, or else a particular point of view. And each one has on occasion at least used every resource at his command to force through Congress the legislative program he espoused. To assume that their successors would abstain from attempting to impose upon their respective administrations a tone complementary to their desires is to assume a purism in politics which is nonexistent. The transfer of quasi-legislative functions to the departmental structure would consequently merely enhance the personal control which the chief executive even now exercises over the government of the United States—and enhance it in fields in which governmental agencies must in the very nature of things be granted broad powers of discretion.

Partly as a protection against personal government, and partly for other reasons it seems imperative to the critics of the proposal advanced by the President's Committee that the regulatory agencies should retain their collegial character. The line of reasoning used in support of the board as over against the purely executive form of administrative organization in connection with these sublegislative activities is, as Blachly and Oatman have indicated, analogous to that used to justify representative government itself: that the legislative product which emanates from a body composed of representatives of diverse political, economic, social, and geographic interests is much more likely to weigh and balance the points of view of these various interests than that which is formulated by a single individual, however well intentioned he may be. For instance, the very diversity of representation on the Federal Reserve Board, drawn as it is from finance, business, and agriculture, and from different geographic regions of the United States, constitutes something of a guarantee that the effect of proposed changes in the Reserve Board's policies upon these various interests will be fully considered before a decision is made. No such guarantee exists, if the decision is concentrated in the hands of a single individual. In the final analysis, the integration of the quasi-legislative functions of the several commissions into the departmental structure would *ipso facto* place them under the control of the chief executive. It may be conceded that, under ordinary circumstances, rule-making by the administration would not mean rule-making by a single individual "but by an entire hierarchy of officers whose successive checks" might be "as effective as the collective efforts of any board." Nevertheless, it may be pointed out in this relation, a board or commission would also, in all probability, receive the comments and memoranda of its own subordinates before arriving at a final decision, and that in fact there is a vital difference between lodging the power of ultimate decision in a single individual and vesting it in a collegial body.

Perhaps the most weighty explanation for the reluctance of these critics to approve the transfer of the administrative and legislative functions of the regulatory authorities to departmental supervision arises from the feeling that the chief executive of the United States is subject to very inadequate legislative and popular control. Such an accretion of power might conceivably foreshadow an ultimate transformation of our political institutions—it might even be a prelude to dictatorship.

On the surface, at least, this fear would appear to be patently absurd, for in both Great Britain and many of the Dominions such quasi-legislative, indeed quasi-judicial bodies are included within the departmental structure. And, as has been indicated previously, similar powers have been conferred upon certain of the departments in the United

States without the destruction of our cherished traditions. It should be pointed out, however, that the powers thus conferred are by contrast to the powers it is proposed to transfer, relatively small. Moreover, the chief executives of both Great Britain and the Dominions are collegial rather than unitary in character. But most important of all, the relation of the executive to the public, and particularly to the legislature, is very different under the British form of government than it is in the United States. The theoretic life of the British executive, if it holds the support of its parliamentary majority, is five years. In fact, the necessity of choosing an opportune moment at which "to go to the country" reduces this period by a number of months. In consequence, the direct control which the electorate may be said to exercise over the chief executive through the medium of popular election is approximately the same in both countries, that is, elections occur about every four years.

The important difference between the status of the two executives is that at any time it so desires the Parliament can refuse further support to the British executive and force its resignation. The fact that such action has been comparatively rare in Great Britain is irrelevant. As the overthrow of the Botha Cabinet in South Africa at the outbreak of the present war strikingly revealed, the power remains. Moreover, even in Great Britain, Parliament has at all times, even in war, continued to influence, if not dominate, Government policies. For instance, in 1935 the Baldwin Ministry felt impelled to sacrifice Sir Samuel Hoare to the outburst of popular resentment which followed the presentation of his Ethiopian policy. Similarly, in 1937 Neville Chamberlain was forced to withdraw his proposed taxes on account of parliamentary criticism from the Opposition and Government benches alike. In other words, by virtue of the continuous dependence of the British executive upon its legislative majority, the members of Parliament can and do exert continuous control over the operation of the government.

Incidentally, partially because of the smaller size of their constituencies and partially because the size of the country enables the members of Parliament to spend their week ends at home, even during a session of Parliament, the British electorate itself, it is frequently asserted, exercises a far greater degree of control over its representatives than does its American counterpart. This indirect pressure is rendered even more effective because of the greater frequency of by-elections under the British system than under the American.

Since the British executive is at all times subject to the control of Parliament and indirectly to that of the electorate, it is possible for those who believe in democratic institutions to view increases in the power of that executive with a greater degree of equanimity than may be warranted in the United States. For this reason the problem of the proper status and situs of the quasi-judicial, quasi-legislative commissions in the administrative structure has never arisen in any acute form in Great Britain. Their obvious place is within the departments.

In striking contrast to the position occupied by the British Cabinet is that occupied by the American President. Save for the difficult and cumbersome process of impeachment, he is assured of continuance in office for a period of four years, with or without the support of a majority in Congress, or even in the country. This lack of legislative control over the occupant of the office of the chief executive in the United States has been largely responsible for the development of itemized budgets, detailed organic acts, pre-audit of administrative expenditures, tenure of office acts, independent commissions, and a number of other devices, all of which are designed to bring the chief executive and the administration under a greater degree of legislative control than would otherwise exist. Those who argue *post hoc, propter hoc* insist that the preservation of American liberties is in no small measure attributable to the ingenuity with which our American legislatures have surmounted this gap in our constitutional system and have harnessed the great leviathan of administration by these devious devices. Needless to say, it is utterly impossible to establish any such direct causal relation, and the argument cannot be taken as at all conclusive.

Nevertheless, the fact remains that the transfer of the administrative and quasi-legislative powers of the regulatory agencies would tremendously enhance the power without in any way strengthening the control over the chief executive. Once granted, these powers, under the veto system, could be legally withdrawn in opposition to the desires of the chief executive only by a two-thirds vote of the Congress, an extraordinary majority difficult to assemble. So, in the opinion of these critics, such an addition of power might reasonably be characterized as a step in the direction of personal government, conceivably as a step in the direction of dictatorship. The fact that a chief executive can, in the course of two terms, appoint a majority of the members of these commissions is only partially relevant. The long and overlapping terms of the commissioners are, to some extent, a guarantee against executive dominance. If they were not, the criticism leveled by the President's Committee against the existing situation would lose much of its force.

Despite the fact that all the constitutional powers of Congress would remain intact legally, the integration of the independent regulatory agencies with the departments would, in the opinion of certain critics, be all the more serious because it would inevitably be accompanied in fact, if not in theory, by a diminution of legislative authority. Indeed, the very minimization of conflict between the commissions and between the commissions and the administration would reduce the frequency of appeals to Congress, and in consequence, congressional influence over these agencies. Moreover, the reconciliation of competing plans relative to public policy within the administration would leave the legislature even more dependent, if possible, upon the executive for the initial formulation of possible solutions for given problems than it is today; the appearance of unity among the experts could hardly fail to buttress still further the already enormous prestige of the chief executive's office.[6]

Such a development would necessarily increase the persuasive or coercive power of the chief executive over the legislature. Although too much credit should not be given to such rumors as those which relate to the indirect purchase of votes by the administration through the allocation of Public Works Administration funds, nevertheless, only a novice in politics assumes that the great game of politics is conducted on the principles laid down in the Golden Rule. If, then, the discretionary powers now exercised by the chief executive are occasionally, perhaps frequently, used to persuade or coerce individual members of Congress into supporting Administration measures, will not a similar use be made of the powers now lodged in the independent commissions, if they are placed under executive control? Despite the vituperations of the executive's critics, the national legislature has in fact never been reduced to a rubber stamp;

[6] To characterize this development as tantamount to the establishment of a dictatorship is, of course, patently absurd, for as long as the powers of election and impeachment continue, and freedom of speech, the press and assembly remain, the ultimate authority will continue to reside in the American people, and the attributes of democracy will continue to characterize the American form of government.

nevertheless, the essentially personal government of Huey Long in the state of Louisiana may in fact foreshadow future developments in the national arena, if too much power is concentrated in the hands of a single individual.

A further consideration, in the opinion of many who assail the proposal of the President's Committee, is the contention that such an organization of the administration might open the way to congressional interference with the work of these regulatory agencies. This, curiously enough, is exactly the obverse of the argument advanced in other quarters. And yet, they hold, it too lies within the realm of possibility. At the present time primary regulatory activities are carried on by agencies which, owing to the commissioners' tenure of office, can neither be reached by the chief executive nor by an ordinary legislative majority—at least not without the chief executive's consent. Their very independence in and of itself calls attention to the quasi-legislative, quasi-judicial aspect of their activities. If they become mere bureaus in the departmental structure, it is argued, such would no longer be the case; both their administrative and quasi-legislative activities would be lost in the routine of run-of-the-mill administration. If senatorial courtesy, as it is rumored, has been sufficiently powerful to force one of the newer agencies not under civil service to allocate forty percent of the jobs at its disposal to the spoilsmen, if the support of the fourteen Senators from the silver states was sufficiently influential to force the administration to acquiesce in a special-interest silver policy, why—the question may well be asked—may not similar legislative pressures dictate the development of the rules and regulations now formulated by these independent agencies—not to mention the granting of exceptions relative thereto? As we have already pointed out, the fact that these items of sublegislation are formulated by agencies independent of executive control makes it impossible for legislative blocks to get at them via the chief executive. And the publicity which inevitably arises from direct attack makes this mode of approach difficult—although, it must be conceded, not impossible. Thus, if the opponents of the proposal are to be believed, the integration of these functions in the departmental structure would inevitably result in an increase in congressional as well as administrative pressure—a consequence devoutly to be avoided.

A supplementary contention of these critics is that it would be impossible to allocate the administrative and quasi-legislative aspect of the work of these agencies to the departments without at the same time giving the department heads a measure of control over the judicial functions as well. In making this assertion, such critics are merely echoing the theory of Blachly and Oatman. Nevertheless, the point is worth elaborating.

Under the proposed scheme of integration, the department head could not, it is true, directly interfere with the adjudication of any case which might come before a judicial section. He could not, for example, compel a judicial section to impose a penalty it did not deem justifiable. The fact remains, however, that under the proposed reform the official initiation of the cases would be transferred from the independent commissions to the departments. Because of this fact, except in those cases in which action can be initiated by private parties, the departments both could and would exert an influence over the judicial sections not only through their refusal to prosecute, but through the manner in which the cases were presented. Thus in the enforcement of the antitrust laws the determination of what constitutes "unfair trade practices" might, in many aspects at least, be determined by the departmental subdivisions carrying on administrative and quasi-legislative work. The mere abstention from prosecution would have the effect of pronouncing a particular trade practice legal—or at least not illegal. It may be asserted, of course, that cases are prepared for the Federal Trade Commission by its administrative subdivision even today. This is true. Nevertheless, the all-pervading influence in the commission is the commissioners, not a politically appointed department head subject to the whims of the chief executive.

But the point may be made that all this is, at bottom, policy determination, not the exercise of a judicial function. The administrative units in the reorganized department, so it is asserted, will bear a relation to the judicial section very similar to that which exists between the prosecutor's office and the courts. This in turn raises a question as to the nature of the prosecutor's office, and suggests calling attention to the fact that, in many jurisdictions at least, the courts are empowered to empanel grand juries without reference to the prosecutor's office. In any event, the enhancement of the chief executive's power contained in the proposal extends so far that, in an extreme situation at least, the judicial sections might practically be abolished, or reduced to inaction, by administrative fiat. Such would certainly be the effect of a complete refusal to prosecute cases before the commissioners.

The truth of the matter is that a differentiation between the administrative, quasi-legislative and quasi-judicial aspects of the work of these commissions is almost impossible except in the realm of theory. In actual practice, "the bulk of the regulatory job is not clearly one thing or another, but a mixture of two or three things. It is a 'mixed' function, combining in the same act elements that are at once policy-determining and judicial."

The general conclusion to which this line of analysis leads is that, even if the criticisms advanced by the exponents of the doctrine of executive management are sound, the proposal for correcting them in and of itself carries so many potential dangers in its train that the cure would appear to be worse than the disease. Such, at least, is the rhetorical statement of the case.

The second major criticism of the independent regulatory agencies emanates from the American Bar Association and is more concerned with the organization and procedure of these agencies than with their independent status. Members of this distinguished professional association believe that the government of the United States is tending in the direction of what they are pleased to call administrative absolutism. This trend is seemingly the inevitable result of a number of undesirable characteristics which have developed in the process of administration during the last several decades. Among those characteristics is the tendency: (1) to decide without a hearing, or without hearing one of the parties; (2) to decide on the basis of matters not before the tribunal or on evidence not produced; (3) to make decisions on the basis of preformed opinions and prejudices; (4) to consider the administrative determining function one of action rather than of decision; (5) to disregard jurisdictional limits and seek to extend the sphere of administrative action beyond the jurisdiction confided to the administrative board or commission; (6) to do what will get by; to yield to political pressure at the expense of the law; (7) to arbitrary rule-making for administrative convenience at the expense of important interests; (8) and, at the other extreme, to fall into a perfunctory routine; (9) to exercise jurisdiction by deputies; and (10) a tendency to mix up rule-making, investigation, prosecution, the advocates' function, the judges' function, and the function of enforcing the judgment, so that the whole proceeding from end to end is one to give effect to a complaint.[7]

These defects, it would appear from the writings of certain members of the Bar Association, inevitably occur "unless the judicial functions of federal administrative tribunals are segregated from their legislative and executive" activities; "unless rules and regulations are made as the result of quasi-judicial procedure and are subject to judicial review; unless principles of common law are applied in the hearing of administrative cases; unless cases involving grants, gratuities, personnel or promotional activities, etc., are handled by the same procedures of hearing and appeal which apply to cases involving regulatory activities; unless there is judicial review over all types of administrative action; and unless the courts have almost complete jurisdiction to pass upon questions of fact as well as questions of law." [8]

The criticisms of the American Bar Association quite obviously are directed to all federal regulatory activity rather than to that which is carried on by the independent regulatory agencies alone. Moreover, in so far as this criticism is applicable to the independent regulatory authorities, it is concentrated upon their organization and procedure, rather than upon their status in the administrative structure. To some extent, however, the two problems are tied together, for the existing organization and procedure of these independent commissions and the independent status allotted to them have all been designed to accomplish a single purpose: the creation of a governmental agency which would be conducive to administrative efficiency and would at the same time respect and protect individual rights guaranteed by law. For this reason, although the discussion may

[7] *Ibid.*, p. 184.
[8] *Ibid.*, p. 185.

appear to be slightly irrelevant to the main purposes of this chapter, an analysis of the criticisms advanced by the Bar Association has a bearing on the processes involved in any administrative reorganization.

In an effort to overcome the objectionable tendencies outlined above, a Special Committee on Administrative Law has drawn up and caused to be introduced into Congress a number of bills designed to correct these defects. Of these, the Walter-Logan Bill is, for our purposes, the most important, for in it the Bar Association not only indicates those aspects of the existing organization and procedure which it considers dangerous to the rights of person and property, but also proposes specific changes designed to correct the deficiencies.

The bill first defines administrative rules as including all rules, regulations, orders, and amendments thereto of general application issued by officers in the executive branch of the United States Government in interpreting the terms of statutes which they are respectively charged with administering. These rules and all amendments thereof, or modifications or supplements of existing rules, are to be issued by the agency concerned only after public notice and hearing, within one year after the enactment of the statute to which they are applicable. Moreover, any person substantially interested in the effects of an administrative rule now in force may petition the head of the appropriate agency to reconsider said rule, and upon the receipt of such a petition the head of such agency shall, after notice and public hearing, determine whether the rule shall be continued in force, be modified, or rescinded.

The United States Court of Appeals for the District of Columbia is to be given authority to hear and determine whether any such rule, issued or continued in force, is in conflict with the Constitution of the United States or the statute under which it was issued. Said Court, however, is to have no power in the proceedings except to render a declaratory judgment holding such rule legal and valid, or holding it contrary to law and invalid.

In addition, by the terms of this bill, the head of every administrative agency shall, from time to time, designate three employees of his agency, at least one of whom shall be a lawyer, for such intra-agency boards as may be necessary. When any person is aggrieved by a decision of any officer or employee of any agency, he may notify the head of the agency in writing, specifically requesting that the controversy be referred to a board. At a time and place to be designated and communicated to the aggrieved person, he shall have an opportunity at an early day for a full and fair hearing before said board. All testimony, other evidence, and all proceedings before the board shall be reduced to writing and filed in the agency concerned. Within thirty days after the argument is closed, the board shall make a written finding of facts and a separate decision thereon—which shall be subject to the written approval, disapproval, or modification of the head of the agency concerned, or of such person as he shall designate in writing to act for him. A copy of the findings of fact and decision, showing the action if any, of the head of the agency concerned, or his representative, shall be filed in the agency, and a copy thereof shall be mailed to the aggrieved person and the intervenors, if any. Any party to such a proceeding, who may be aggrieved by the final decision or order of any agency may, within thirty days after the receipt of a copy thereof, file a written petition with the United States Court of Appeals for the District of Columbia, or with an appropriate circuit court of appeals, for review of the decision. Said court may affirm or set aside the decision or may direct the agency concerned to modify its decision. Moreover, a case may, in the discretion

172 ADMINISTRATIVE REGULATION

of the courts, be remanded to the agency in which it arose
for the development of further evidence.

Any decision or any agency or independent agency shall be
set aside if it is made to appear to the satisfaction of the
court (1) that the findings of fact are clearly erroneous;
or (2) that the findings of fact are not supported by sub-
stantial evidence; or (3) that the decision is not supported
by the findings of fact; or (4) that the decision was issued
without due notice and a reasonable opportunity having been
afforded the aggrieved party for a full and fair hearing; or
(5) that the decision is beyond the jurisdiction of the
agency or the independent agency, as the case may be; or
(6) that the decision infringes the Constitution or statutes
of the United States; or (7) that the decision is otherwise
contrary to law.

The judgments of the circuit court of appeals shall be
final, except that they shall be subject to review by the
Supreme Court of the United States upon writ of certiorari
of certification.[9]

This, in broad outline, is the proposal of the American

[9] The final paragraph of the bill remains to be noted: Nothing contained in this Act shall apply to or affect any matter concerning or
relating to the conduct of military or naval operations; the trial by
courts martial of persons otherwise within the jurisdiction of such
courts martial; the conduct of the Federal Reserve Board, the Office
of the Comptroller of the Currency, the Federal Deposit Insurance
Corporation, the Federal Trade Commission, the Interstate Commerce Commission, the conduct of the Department of State; the conduct of the Department of Justice and the offices of the United States
attorneys, except as otherwise herein specifically provided; or any
matter concerning or relating to the internal revenue, customs, patent,
trademark, copyright, or longshoremen and harbor workers' laws; or
any case where the aggrieved party was denied a leave, or may be
dissatisfied with a grading in the connection with the purchase or sale
of agricultural products, or has failed to receive appointment or employment by any agency or independent agency. Sections 2 and 3 of
this Act shall not apply to the General Accounting Office.

Bar Association to correct the deficiencies in administrative organization and procedure which are, in its opinion, causing the Government of the United States to tend toward administrative absolutism.

Thus, far from being impressed by the argument of the President's Committee for a greater degree of executive control, the members of the Bar Association are seemingly alarmed by the extent to which, in both the independent agencies and the departmental structures, private rights are, at the moment, being subordinated to administrative convenience and dominance.

To correct the situation, the members of the Special Committee on Administrative Law propose the establishment of a procedure which will set forth once and for all and within a period of one year the rules and regulations by which conduct is to be guided; the establishment of a quasi-judicial procedure within each agency with authority not merely over adjudicatory activity, but administrative and legislative as well; and finally the further subordination of this regulatory activity to judicial review. In so far as one can tell it is a matter of indifference to the Bar Association whether the independent regulatory agencies thus reorganized and subjected to judicial control are incorporated in the departmental structure or not. Nor is there any reason they should be, for if the recommendations of the Bar Association are accepted, the effective control of these commissions will be lodged in the courts—and the desire of the exponents of the doctrine of executive management to bring them under executive dominance will have been completely frustrated.

The proposal of the American Bar Association has consequently evoked vigorous dissent from the exponents of executive management and the defenders of the *status quo* alike. It is pointed out in the first place that it is simply impossible for the administration to implement once and for all many of the statutes passed by Congress within a year after enactment. So long as Congress continues to lay down such vague and complex standards as "reasonable rates," "public convenience and necessity," "unreasonable discrimination," "undue preference," "adequate facilities and services," "maintenance of a fair and orderly market," "unfair methods of competition," "collective bargaining," "unfair labor practices," and the like, the implementation of these statutes must of necessity be a continuous process. Thus, to use a concrete example, "reasonable railroad rates" today might become exceedingly unreasonable by 1950, if in the interim there occurred a radical inflation. Similarly, the maintenance of "adequate facilities and services" as of the year 1940 might impose an altogether unreasonable burden upon these same enterprises by the year 1950, if automobile and air transport continue to make inroads into railroad traffic similar to those which they have made in the past.

Second, in the opinion of these critics it seems highly improbable that adequate rules or regulations can be formulated solely through the procedure of public hearings. Inevitably, on account of the technical and highly complicated character of modern administration, minor adjustments are continually necessary. Under the Walter-Logan Bill these could be made only after public notice and hearing—a process necessarily productive of delay, and one which would increase the burden of administration many times. Special interests primarily bent on the maintenance of the *status quo* could without question use the procedure in such a fashion as to hamper, if not to cripple, the processes of administration. In so much as public hearings are very likely to become a forum preëminently for the defense of private interests, it is highly probable that the public interest would be more easily lost to sight under the Bar Association plan than it is under the present procedure. Furthermore, since the ultimate control of administrative decisions would be transferred from the administration to the courts presided over by judges who have been much more thoroughly trained in the principles of the law than they have in administration, the administrative factors involved in each situation would doubtless be given less weight than they really merit.

Incidentally, it may be noted in passing, the Bar Association Bill would impose upon the courts a task which they have hitherto shrunk from as involving a violation of the principle of separation of powers as it is embodied, or more accurately, implied, in the Constitution; to wit, judicial control over the exercise of purely administrative discretion.

Third, the proposal to establish intra-agency boards is criticized on the grounds that (a) the functions of the administrative agencies encompassed by the Bill are so extremely varied that "they cannot reasonably be subjected to a single type of procedure and control" and that (b) since no limitation has been placed upon the character of the controversy in which an appeal may be taken, the inevitable result will be a totally unnecessary complication of the process of administration to the point that it may conceivably break down.

This criticism has a bearing on the proposal as applied to the operation of the independent regulatory agencies despite the provision in the measure for initial action by a trial examiner; for, in the final analysis, the requirement that, when an objection has been filed against the decision of the trial examiner, a public hearing shall be held before three members of the commission before final action is taken, is for all practical purposes a slight variation of the same procedural requirement.

Finally, in the opinion of the critics of the proposal, the

Bar Association's Bill imposes upon the courts the duty of reviewing not merely law but also fact in connection with each controversy appealed. As an almost inevitable result, the court will on occasion at least substitute its judgment for that of the administrative and quasi-administrative officers, when "as a practical matter the judiciary is no more fitted to enter the specialized fields of public administration, nor endowed with the technical competence necessary to solve the intricate problems arising in connection with the enforcement of modern legislative policies, than are the legislative bodies which were forced to delegate such functions to specialized tribunals." [10]

Thus exponents of the doctrine of executive management and defenders of the *status quo* unite to denounce the proposal of the American Bar Association so to reorganize and transform the existing organization and procedure of the independent commissions as to subordinate them to judicial control as fundamentally unsound in its conception, and disastrous to efficient administration in its execution.

Although the two proposals we have just been discussing have undoubtedly received the most widespread publicity, two other concepts as to the proper organization and status of the independent regulatory authorities deserve notice.

The first of these, emanating from the Brookings Institution, has been labeled by proponents the revisionist doctrine. To its adherents, the multiplicity and diversity of the activities now being carried on by the independent agencies render it highly improbable that a simple, universally applicable formula relative to either their status, organization or procedure, will ever be discovered. As the revisionists see it, this fact disposes of all administrative "reformers," for, as

---

[10] "Administrative Justice and the Rule of Discretion," 47 *Yale Law Journal*, 597. Quoted by Blachly and Oatman, *op. cit.*, p. 226.

they survey the existing scene, "the present system of federal administration [is] a vast complex organization . . . carefully devised to combine the protection of guaranteed rights with the promotion of administrative efficiency. The constitutional and statutory bases of administration, the forms of administrative action, the enforcement methods and controls applicable to the respective forms, and the special devices for obtaining efficiency contribute to both these ends. The system is not perfect; but it is constantly being improved as to efficiency; at the same time its operations are devised and controlled in such a way that guaranteed rights are safeguarded." [11]

The revisionists consequently stand foursquare for the maintenance and preservation of the broad outlines of the existing system, emphasizing particularly the necessity for maintaining the independence of all agencies which are carrying out long-term regulatory processes.

But if the revisionists are conservatives, they are not against all changes in administration. It is their belief that considerable improvement can be made in the present administrative system, without in any way destroying administrative efficiency, in (1) the forms of administrative action, (2) administrative procedures, (3) the enforcement of administrative acts, and (4) control over administrative action.

The first step in the direction of desirable change, as they see it, is a clarification of the language of the statutes with regard to the forms of administrative action and a correlation of necessary procedural requirements with the character of the action taken. To this end they suggest that "the expression 'rules and regulations' be reserved for general sublegislative norms made under statutory authorization" and that the enactment of such rules and regulations be left free

[11] *Ibid.,* p. 266.

from statutory prescription; that the word "decision" should be confined to "administrative actions of a discretionary nature" and that acts of this character should be subjected to judicial review only to the extent of controlling abuses of power and *ultra vires* actions. The multitude of actions now covered by the term "order" should, in the opinion of the revisionists, be clearly differentiated. Procedural or interlocutory orders should be so designated, and should not "be subjected to any special procedure as regards issuance," or to judicial review.

Legislative regulatory orders, it should be recognized, fall into three main categories: (1) those "which resemble a rule or regulation in that they are general in nature and implement or supplement the law directly"; (2) those "which although legislative in nature, directly affect the right of individuals"; and (3) those "which, though they do not immediately affect rights, may serve as a basis for future action which does affect rights." As the revisionists see it, judicial review over orders falling in the first and third categories should be confined to questions of *ultra vires* action and abuse of power; but orders which fall into the second category should be subjected to rigid control. Such orders should be issued only after notice and hearing, and should be based on the evidence brought forward at the hearing. Actions of this character should obviously be subjected to judicial review both as to law and fact.

Such a clarification of the terminology of the statutes and correlation of the necessary procedural requirement with the character of the action taken would, in the opinion of the revisionists, go a long way to clearing up much of the confusion which at the present time befuddles the thinking in connection with the regulatory activities of the federal government.

The second major step in the program advanced by the

revisionists relates to the problem of procedure. Although, in their opinion, the diversity of activities of the federal administration makes impossible the establishment of a single type of procedure applicable to all situations, certain procedural principles can be established. As the preceding paragraphs have indicated, it seems to the revisionists self-evident that general regulatory orders which have a wide and nonspecific field of application—which are, in other words, essentially legislative in their character—should not be hedged in with rigid procedural requirements, nor subjected to judicial review beyond that customarily imposed upon all statutes.

The specific administrative order, however, falls into a different classification. Here the revisionists see eye to eye with the courts in insisting that such orders be issued only after notice and hearing, and that the orders be based upon the facts brought out at such hearings. Nevertheless, even here the revisionists would make an exception; cease and desist orders belong in a separate category, one in which the administrators should be granted a greater degree of freedom than is possible under the procedural requirements now imposed.

Perhaps the most radical change in the existing organization proposed by them is the establishment of a Court of Appeals for Administration. Through the creation of such an agency, they argue, it would be possible to introduce a much higher degree of uniformity into judicial rulings on administrative matters than is conceivable in a situation in which one hundred different courts hand down separate opinions. The development of a greater uniformity in judicial determinations would obviously clarify the processes of administration still further. Moreover, by virtue of its specialization, such a Court should shortly attain an ability to achieve that balance between the necessities of efficient administration and the protection of guaranteed rights which is essential to the process of government in the modern era—a balance, incidentally, which judges grounded in the common law, steeped in the tradition that it is the primary function of the courts to protect private rights, all too frequently fail to achieve.

It is evident, from what has been said above, that the exponents of the revisionist doctrine agree neither with the line of reasoning pursued by the President's Committee on Administrative Management, nor with that followed by the American Bar Association. Instead, they accept, in large measure, the system as it exists at the present day, and have concentrated their efforts on improving the technicalities of its operation—not on destroying its structure.

A fourth, and for purposes of this discussion final, concept of the disposition of the independent regulatory agencies is advanced by those who might be called eclectic in their outlook. Taking cognizance of the criticisms of the existing system contained in the analysis of the President's Committee on Administrative Management, the American Bar Association and the Brookings Institution, the adherents of this concept note that each of these agencies has emphasized only one aspect of the total structure. The President's Committee on Administrative Management, for example, was forced by its very terms of reference to concentrate on the problem of over-all executive management. An understanding with the Brookings Institution compelled the committee to leave relatively unexplored a problem as closely related as that of departmentalization. The American Bar Association, on account of its professional characteristics, is seemingly primarily interested in the protection of private rights. The fact that its proposal substantially increases the amount of legal and justiciable work involved in the administration of regulatory legislation can be passed over as irrelevant. Although the work of the Brookings Institution is apparently somewhat broader in its scope, including as it does an analysis of the proposals of both the President's Committee on Administrative Management and the American Bar Association, its conclusions suggest that it started with and ended with a general approval of the *status quo*—subject, of course, to the minor modifications indicated above.

This fixation upon one aspect of a situation rather than upon the entire problem of administration in relation to the critical state of popular government today appears to the eclectics an exceedingly dangerous form of astigmatism which prevents its victims from seeing the woods because of the trees.

To those who believe that the part is inseparable from the whole, it seems imperative that before any drastic action is taken an attempt be made to survey and appraise the whole situation, as far as that is at present possible. Such a survey would include more than an analysis of the situation from the point of view of executive management, or with reference to an interest in the protection of vested interests, or on the assumption that the *status quo* is excellent except for matters of technique. It would, instead, extend to the whole range of governmental, political, economic, and social activities which are now actually in process of radical change, and which might be affected by any contemplated alteration in administration. It would neither boldly assert that its conclusions "were based on no assumption," [12] nor mask its assumptions in a mass of persiflage about human liberty, without ever becoming specific as to whose liberty is involved or as to the purpose to which such liberty is dedicated. Instead, such a survey would quite consciously examine the assumptions and presuppositions upon the basis

[12] *Ibid.*, p. 231.

of which it proposed to erect an administrative superstructure. It might conceivably conclude that the basic assumptions and presuppositions of the past were entirely sound; more likely, it would conclude that the changing circumstances of the modern world had rendered some modifications imperative. In any event, it would boldly set forth the postulates from which it intended to proceed.

Although in the absence of such a survey it is, of course, impossible to state definitively what its conclusions might be, a number of things appear to be highly probable. First, it seems reasonably certain that some form of capitalistic economy and political democracy will endure in the United States. This assumption has, of course, at least two implications relevant to the problem at hand: the continued existence of private property and of vested interests in that property; and the continued subordination of our system of government to popular control. Second, in view of the problems arising out of the Great Depression and the accompanying rise of the totalitarian economies, it seems highly probable that the degree of governmental control over our economic life will increase rather than decrease; larger and larger areas of our economy will become involved in governmental guidance, bolstering, and planning. Third, owing to the increasing responsibilities of government, the tendency toward executive leadership in the formulation and initiation of public policy can be expected to accelerate rather than to disappear. Fourth, this increase in executive power, all other things remaining the same, means a corresponding decrease in legislative power, and, to some extent at least, in popular control over governments, unless the legislature proves to be more effective in devising policies and measures than it has been in recent years.

Accepting, as they do, these confessedly unverified assumptions, the eclectics deem it self-evident that the proper organization of the independent regulatory agencies and their allocation to the most desirable places in the administrative structure involves not one but at least three inseparable problems. First is their relation to the chief executive; second, the protection of individual rights; and third, hitherto neglected in the discussion of the subject, the implementation of legislative control over the executive and the administration.

As we might expect, eclectics are very much impressed with the criticism advanced by the President's Committee concerning the confusion and lack of coördination—both in matters of administration and public policy—arising from the independence of the regulatory commissions; moreover, it seems obvious that further multiplication of such agencies will increase rather than diminish this confusion. They are also impressed, however, by the multiplicity and diversity of the commissions' activities. It seems to them, consequently, that the functioning of these several agencies deserves individual study and that the final decision as to their proper place in the administrative structure must be made in each individual case, rather than upon the basis of some single, simple, universally applicable formula. The latter procedure, in the opinion of the eclectics, is open to the objection that lies against the *a priori* method in general. Unless a solid case can be made for independence, however, the exponents of eclecticism would be inclined to argue with the President's Committee that these independent agencies should be incorporated in the departmental structure. The degree of their incorporation, however, would not necessarily be uniform; instead, it would vary according to the exigencies of each particular case.

The American Bar Association, like the President's Committee on Administrative Management, has fallen into the error of prescribing a single simple formula for all complications, one which, in the opinion of the eclectics, would complicate the process of administration to the point of paralysis. This is not equivalent to saying that no further steps in the protection of private rights are needed. Quite the contrary, the exponents of the doctrine of eclecticism are in full agreement with the Brookings Institution in regard to the desirability both of clarifying the terminology of the statutes and prescribing by statute procedural requirements correlative to the type of discretion delegated. The possibilities of a Court of Appeals for Administration should certainly be thoroughly explored.

No less important is it, from the point of view of the eclectics, that ways and means be discovered for implementing the legislature's control over the administration. As long as Congress retains control over appropriations, the ultimate power of policy-determination will continue to reside in the legislative body. Nevertheless, as was indicated above, the transfer of the independent regulatory authorities to the departmental structure will *ipso facto* increase the power of the chief executive. And, unless at the same time steps are taken to counteract it, it will decrease the power of the legislature. Consequently, before any such drastic action is taken, the eclectics consider it imperative to investigate the existing organization and procedure of Congress with a view to discovering whether radical improvements could not be made in the organization, procedure, and staffing of the standing committees so that they might operate as much more efficient instrumentalities of administrative supervision than they do at the present time. In this respect a lesson might conceivably be drawn from the British question hour and from the French Parliamentary Commissions for adaptation to American usage. The potentialities of a further extension of the system of provisional orders might be explored. And the possibility of improving the operations of

Congressional investigating committees examined. Some attention might be given to the desirability of establishing an American counterpart to the Parliamentary Committee on Accounts. The important thing, from the eclectics' point of view, is not the particular device which might be used to increase the effectiveness of Congressional supervision over the administration, but the fact that some technique or set of techniques must be evolved to accomplish this purpose. And the wholesale transfer of the independent regulatory agencies to the department should not be consummated until these techniques are in actual operation.

In this fashion, and in this fashion alone, do those who subscribe to the eclectic doctrine believe that it is possible to arrive at a better working solution of the problem raised by the development of independent regulatory agencies in modern government.

Whatever the merits of this controversy, one thing is obvious—the study of public administration has not as yet evolved any generally accepted scientific principles capable of automatic application to the problem of the organization and status of the independent regulatory agencies. Instead, four different concepts of organization contend for supremacy. Each of these concepts is based upon a major premise or presupposition, some times articulate, some times inarticulate. And upon each premise is built an entire superstructure of administrative theory designed to achieve the objectives its exponents have in mind. Quite obviously, as we have said previously, the points of conflict relative to administrative organization do not lie wholly within the field of administrative organization itself. Instead, they ramify not merely throughout the whole governmental organization, but throughout the political, social, and economic order as well.

VII ✦ ✦

INTERDEPARTMENTAL INTEGRATION

IMPELLING AS ARE THE REASONS FOR THE DEPARTMENTAL-
ization of the administrative structure of modern government,
no less imperative is the necessity for interdepartmental
integration. Historically, the agency which has exercised
this function has been the Cabinet or, under the Constitution of the United States, the chief executive himself.
More recently certain supplementary over-all agencies have
developed with this same end in view, although for limited
purposes.

INSTITUTIONALIZED CONTROL

Although we are not, in this volume, primarily concerned
with the *raison d'être* of these new over-all agencies but
rather with their place in the administrative structure, a
brief survey of recent developments is pertinent to the theme
of this book. For the most part these agencies fall into three
categories: service, managerial, and planning.

That, in many situations, specific activities common to all
departments such as purchasing, the allocation of office
space, printing, etc., can be handled more effectively upon
a centralized rather than a departmental basis has long since
been demonstrated.[1] Distinct economies which are attain-

---

[1] A word of caution is, perhaps, necessary. Although centralized
purchasing is highly desirable for governmental units located in a particular governmental area, it would become intolerable if an attempt
were made to extend the practice throughout the length and breadth
of the governmental structure. Units of government scattered from
Tokyo to Berlin simply must be allowed a high degree of autonomy.

able only through the consolidation of departmental requisitions can be secured by large scale purchases. Moreover, where the supply of an article is limited or the mechanism of production inadequate, as in the case of certain types of armaments, a system of priorities can frequently be worked out which will certainly minimize the intensity of interdepartmental competition and may, in fact, largely eliminate the disadvantages inherent in this competition. Centralized control over the leasing of office space not only permits the allocation and re-allocation of government owned quarters as the fluctuating needs of the departments may dictate, but it may also prevent the unnecessary leasing of space in privately owned buildings where governmental facilities are available. Under certain circumstances, such as those which exist in Washington today, centralized printing may not only eliminate the duplication by the departments of expensive equipment and a highly paid personnel, but duplication by the legislature as well. Similarly, centralized library and archive service not only prevents excessive duplication in library purchases and personnel, but also facilitates the work of the administration, the legislature, and the general public alike.

Further illustrations are unnecessary. The important point is that, in a highly complicated administrative organization, the need for centralized service agencies is generally, if not universally, conceded. Only by means of over-all agencies of this character is it possible to administer most efficiently a large number of service activities which are common to all, or at least to a majority of, the units into which the administration is divided.

In a somewhat different category are those activities which are essentially managerial in character. Of these the reorganization of the administrative structure of government, the selection of personnel, the formulation of the budget, reporting, direction, and control are, perhaps, the most important. In a very small organization these activities may all be carried on by a single individual. This becomes increasingly difficult, however, with the growth in size and complexity of the administrative units until finally two courses of action only are open—the decentralization of these managerial functions along departmental lines with an increasing dependence upon "the dominance of a common idea" or *esprit de corps* as the great integrating force, or the development of a number of over-all agencies designed to exercise these functions.

Both of these procedures have been followed. Historically, however, the former has usually taken precedence over the latter.

Thus control over staffing or personnel in the federal administration was originally conceived to be primarily a matter of departmental concern. And even today, the State, Army, and Navy services are selected almost exclusively upon this basis, as is also the personnel of the United States Public Health Service, the Coast and Geodetic Survey, the Coast Guard, and a number of other subordinate administrative units. Nor is this peculiarly an American phenomenon. In Fascist Italy, for example, the selection of the administrative personnel is entirely under the control of the several departments, subject of course to the pressure of the Fascist Party. The passage of the Pendleton Act by the Congress of the United States in 1883 marks not only a major step in the minimization of the spoils system in the United States, but—equally important—a recognition of the advantages of centralized personnel control. Although the merit system is, in fact, not universally accepted in the federal administration even today, in so far as it is, the administration thereof has, with the exceptions noted, been largely concentrated in the hands of a centralized agency.

Similarly, the preparation of budget estimates in the United States was, historically, largely a matter of departmental concern. This was as true of the federal administration as it was of state and municipal governments. Participation by the chief executive in the preparation of these estimates was, for the most part, confined to items in which he had a personal interest, to proposals which necessitated the enactment of new nonbudgetary legislation, and to such other matters as the department heads might deem it wise to call to his attention. For the rest, his function was largely the transmission of the departmental requests to the legislature. Despite an historic aversion to the centralization of power, the disadvantages of this piecemeal budgetary procedure finally led to the Budget and Accounting Act of 1921.

Since that date, requests for appropriations are routed to a central fiscal agency, the Budget Bureau, before going either to the chief executive or to Congress. Specialists attached to the Budget Bureau both coördinate and analyze these departmental requests in such a way as to make possible something approximating a rounded picture of the financial operations of the federal government. Nor is the development in any way unique. This increasing centralization of financial control in the hands of the chief executive is not, needless to say, a peculiar characteristic of the federal government, nor is it confined to the governmental units of the United States. Instead, it is a world-wide phenomenon.

Somewhat similar in its basic concept is the recent endeavor to establish a centralized system of clearance for governmental reporting in general. Until recently reports on administrative actions or policies—other than financial—were largely made through the medium of the annual reports of the various administrative agencies, reports from interdepartmental committees which had been set up to work out particular problems, reports from certain over-all agencies such as the Budget Bureau, the National Resources Committee, etc., and special reports relative to particular problems which had attracted the chief executive's attention. But not until the creation of the National Emergency Council did an agency exist which had as its *raison d'être* the analysis, synthesis, and interpretation of the nonfiscal information which ordinarily flows from the administration to the chief executive. Although the work of the National Emergency Council cannot be said to have been a striking success, the transfer of its functions to the White House staff and the inadequacy of the previous system of reporting both suggest that we are witnessing the beginning of a further managerial agency dedicated to introducing into the field of administrative reporting generally something of the order and clarity which has characterized fiscal reporting since the establishment of the Bureau of the Budget in 1921.

Until recently, in so far as the power of organization was delegated to the federal administrative authorities at all, it was delegated to the heads of particular departments. Thus the Secretary of State was given relatively complete control over the internal organization of the Department of State. And to a lesser degree similar powers of administrative organization were conferred upon the Secretary of Agriculture. Elsewhere in the administration the grant of organic power has been distinctly limited. In no case, however, did these various grants of power make possible interdepartmental reorganization.

Only within recent times have a number of attempts been made to implement the office of the chief executive in this direction, although the results of these efforts have not been particularly effective. Thus in 1913 the Bureau of Efficiency was established for the purpose of studying both administrative organization and administrative procedure. Due to the exigencies of the World War, an even more sweeping grant of power was conferred upon President Wilson. The terms of the Overman Act, however, were narrowly construed as being primarily applicable to military or wartime purposes. The first broad grant of authority to the chief executive relative to the consolidation and re-allocation of administrative agencies in time of peace, consequently, was conferred upon Herbert Hoover in June, 1932. In fairness to Mr. Hoover it should be noted that this authority was conferred upon him while he was in the middle of a desperate political campaign, and that it was subject to congressional veto. It is not surprising, consequently, that Mr. Hoover made no attempt to exercise these powers until some six months later, nor is it particularly astonishing to hear that the House vetoed Mr. Hoover's proposals in order to give the incoming President a free hand in connection with the problems with which he was confronted. A still further grant of authority to reorganize the administrative structure of the government was conferred in 1932 upon Franklin Roosevelt who, however, failed to make any extensive use of the power during the first four years of his administration.

Despite the failure of the chief executives effectually to use the organic power thus conferred upon them, and despite the uproar which greeted the original proposal for a renewal of that grant in 1937, the exigencies of public business compelled Congress to confer upon the President much more radical powers of administrative reorganization than Presidents have been accustomed to possess, except under the emergency circumstances previously noted. By virtue of this recent grant of power, a number of shifts in the administrative organization have already been made, and, much more important from the point of view of our discussion, an over-all agency has been established, the function of which is the further analysis of administrative organization and procedure from the point of view both of efficiency and economy.

In this connection, incidentally, it is relevant to note that although in theory no such grant of authority has been conferred upon the chief executives of either England or France, such authority exists in fact. The almost complete mastery exercised by the British Cabinet over the House of Commons inevitably means that the members of that House are at all times confronted with the necessity either of acquiescing in any changes in the administrative structure the Cabinet may suggest, or, if the Cabinet so desires, of precipitating an election. How utterly inconceivable it is that an election could be precipitated upon such an issue is revealed by the fact that at the present time many if not a majority of the subordinate units of British administration rest upon the basis of an executive ordinance rather than upon statute. In consequence the British Cabinet may be said to possess at all times, in fact if not in theory, powers fully commensurate with those temporarily possessed by President Hoover and by President Roosevelt in 1933 and very much greater than those conferred upon the President by the legislation of 1937. Similarly, although the French Cabinet exercises no such dominance over the French Parliament as does its British counterpart in Great Britain, the French Parliament has usually acquiesced, without raising grave disturbances, in all changes in administrative organization that the Cabinet has proposed. Thus, in this relation, European developments have foreshadowed the course of events here.

Until comparatively recently, no impelling necessity for implementing the chief executive's power of direction—i.e., "the continuous task of making decisions and embodying them in specific and general orders and instructions and serving as the leader of the enterprise"—seems to have arisen in either the federal government or in the states. Instead, quite satisfactory results seem to have been attainable along departmental lines. In those countries operating under the cabinet system this has been largely due to the fact that the heads of the various departments have themselves been constituent parts of the executive. In the United States it may be attributed to the fact that the major managerial contacts of the President long numbered only ten. They were, in consequence, or were thought to be, well within the chief executive's span of control. The increasing difficulty and complexity of British administration during the troublesome days of the first World War, however, gave impetus to the implementation of the British executive in this direction. A cabinet secretariat was established both for the purpose of expediting interdepartmental coördination and facilitating the direction of various ministerial activities. The increasing complexities of administration under the New Deal have stimulated analogous proposals here. These have finally resulted in the grant of authority to the chief executive to appoint six administrative assistants to help him in his managerial functions. Just what form this American secretariat will take is not as yet entirely clear.

Of quite a different character from either of these service or managerial aids are the planning agencies which have been suggested from time to time. Their *raison d'être* is neither to facilitate the housekeeping functions of government nor to manage or direct. Their purpose, as their designation indicates, is that of planning and advising, suggesting and recommending.

The planning concept is largely the outgrowth of military experience, the product of a growing realization that pressure of a multitude of administrative duties makes it virtually impossible for the commanding officer of any large military establishment to obtain the leisure and the information necessary to think through or plan alternative strategies. In consequence, in the military sphere at least, the problem of planning has largely been delegated to an agency specifically created for this purpose—the general staff. The ultimate decision is still within the prerogative of the commander in chief. The function of the planning agency is merely to advise, suggest, or recommend.

From its creation in 1933 The National Planning Board, now the National Resources Planning Board, has been the nearest institutional approximation to such an agency on the civilian side of the federal administration. Its activities, however, were by virtue of its terms of reference somewhat limited. Its transfer to the White House in 1939 may quite possibly forecast its transformation into a real over-all planning agency.

With the growing complexity of administration it becomes apparent that a number of service, general managerial, and planning functions of government can be more effectively handled through the medium of administrative units whose authority cuts across and in some respects supersedes departmental lines. The point at which these diverse activities should assume institutional form varies from situation to situation and might well constitute a study by itself.

From the point of view of departmentalization, the important problem is the relation which these over-all agencies should bear to each other and the place they should occupy in the administrative structure.

Four divergent concepts relative to the proper location of these administrative units seem to be current at the moment. In the first place, they might all be given a status in the administrative structure *independent both of the departments and of each other*. Second, they might all be grouped in an executive department headed either by a cabinet officer or by the chief executive himself. Third, they might all be allocated to the Treasury, which would thus become not merely a fiscal unit but a managerial agency as well. Finally, each of these over-all units might be considered individually, and allocated to that position in the administrative structure, *whether within the departments or independent of them,* which its peculiar characteristics seem to dictate.

The argument for granting each of these units an independent status comparable to that now occupied by the Civil Service Commission may be summarized briefly. Each of these agencies—those who believe in this pattern of organization point out—encompasses within the scope of its jurisdiction functions which cut across departmental lines. Consequently, to integrate any one of them into the departmental structure would give rise to jealousy, irritation, and charges of departmental favoritism. For example, the allocation of office space and the procurement of supplies were formerly subject, in part at least, to the Departments of the Interior and the Treasury respectively, a fact which again and again evoked charges of departmental favoritism, particularly in connection with the assignment of office space and to a lesser extent in connection with the delivery of supplies. If the other service agencies which are now independent—the Library of Congress, the National Archives, the Government Printing Office, etc.—were likewise integrated into the departmental structure similar criticism might be expected. The fact that the latter agencies are designed for congressional and public use as well as for the use of administrative officials would, in all probability, intensify rather than minimize the dissatisfaction. Rational or irrational, the truth is that even the slight degree of control, if such it can be called, which is exercised by the service agencies offends the *amour propre* of the various departments, if the agency involved is subordinate to a sister department.

The situation, in the opinion of those who favor an independent status for these agencies, is even more aggravated in the case of the managerial and planning agencies whose functions not only transcend departmental lines, but frequently come into direct conflict with both departmental traditions and aspirations. The Budget Bureau does of necessity pare down departmental requests for appropriations; the Civil Service Commission dictates the broad outlines of personnel policy. The allocation of these to one or more departments would, consequently, produce interdepartmental irritation and encourage a determination on the part of the other departments to defend their departmental prerogatives and independence at all costs. The hostility which former Secretary Henry A. Wallace was at one time said to hold toward the National Resources Committee, which had its beginnings under the P. W. A., may serve to illustrate the point. According to reports, Secretary Wallace held the opinion that the National Resources Committee was being used by the Department of Interior to advance Secretary Ickes' aspirations to head a Department of Conservation.

Efforts on the part of nonmanagerial departments to protect themselves from the dominance of departments having managerial units would result in interdepartmental discord and an increase in the managerial burden carried by the over-all agencies. Certainly this would offset any advantage that might accrue from their integration in the departmental structure—a discord, incidentally, which could be avoided by granting these agencies an independent status.

The inclusion of over-all managerial and planning units in the departmental structure, moreover, would of necessity mean that the chief executive's orders and directions to them would filter through the head of the department in which they had been incorporated, and would, in consequence, be subject to his interpretation. Thus, if the managerial units were located in the Treasury, an executive order relative to the more effective coördination of the relief activities, filtering through the Secretary of the Treasury, might easily be given a financial slant; the chief emphasis would then be upon increased economy rather than increased service to the recipients of relief, when the latter rather than the former was intended. Similarly, if the division of administrative organization were located in a given department, any addition to the scope of that department's work would be viewed with the suspicion that it was due more largely to departmental pressure than to the logic of the situation. In any event, the possibility that such pressure might be exerted would undoubtedly give rise to charges that it had been exercised, an incidental result of which might very easily be frequent appeals over the heads of the managerial and planning agency to the chief executive himself. More important —in so far as the heads of these managerial departments did take it upon themselves to interpret executive orders—they would be arrogating to themselves a function which, in the opinion of many, is, or at least should be, the exclusive pre-rogative of the chief executive, i.e., the final decision in determining the broad outline of administrative policy. Here, too, consequently, difficulties could be avoided by granting these agencies an independent status.

Inevitably the question will arise: Why should not these various agencies be grouped into a single agency or department immediately under the chief executive? The question will be discussed at length later. Suffice it to say for the moment, that in the eyes of those who favor the assignment of these agencies to an autonomous status, the lack of any great natural interrelation between them precludes the possibility of attaining increased administrative efficiency in this fashion. Thus, in their opinion, the relation of the Budget Bureau to the Government Printing Office or the Congressional Library is no more intimate than it is to other units of government picked at random. Illustrations might be multiplied, but the final conclusion would be the same; there is no peculiar interrelationship between service, managerial, and planning units which would justify their integration into a single establishment. Hence, it would appear that a status at once independent of the departmental structure and of one another will enable them to function at a maximum of efficiency with the least administrative irritation or interference.

This conclusion has, of course, evoked vigorous dissent. The independent status of these agencies would necessarily increase rather than diminish the supervisory burden imposed upon the chief executive, for the heads of these various independent establishments would presumably have direct access to him. To some extent, consequently, this form of organization would undermine one of the main objectives of the entire process of departmentalization, i.e., the reduction of the number of direct managerial contacts with the chief executive to the point that the remaining contacts fall within his span of control. True, the work of certain of these units—for example, the Library of Congress and National Archives—is at once so routine and so technical in character that the number of questions which would be brought to the attention of the chief executive might be negligible and the amount of time consumed slight. Such, however, would not be the case with other agencies, particularly those concerned with planning, budgeting, and personnel. In connection with each of these, conferences would of necessity be frequent and lengthy, involving in many cases the coördination of the activities of the planning and managerial units with the activities of certain of the departments, or with each other.

For, as the dissenters view the situation, the activities of certain of these agencies are not only mutually interrelated, but are also closely connected with the work of the Treasury itself. The operation of the Budget Bureau, for example, impinges at many points on that of the Civil Service Commission. And certainly it is difficult to conceive of anything other than an intimate relationship between this fiscal unit and any agency which may be developed for the improvement either of the administrative organization or administrative procedures. In fact, so intimate was this relationship deemed by the present Administration that the recently created division of administrative management has been made an integral part of the Bureau of the Budget itself. In similar fashion, the work of this latter division or agency will be intimately connected with that of the Civil Service Commission or any agency which may be substituted for it. Although it is perfectly true that the degree of interrelationship between certain of the service agencies is slight, such is not the case between others. Therefore the allocation of the various agencies to an independent status would, so it is urged, in no way reduce the intolerable administrative burden upon the chief executive. On the contrary, it might conceivably add to it.

A second method of handling the several service, managerial, and planning agencies would be to group them together in an executive department or office headed by a Cabinet officer or an Under Secretary immediately subordinate to the President. In such an event, it is argued, the coördination of their routine activities could easily be handled by a Secretary or Under Secretary as the case might be. Their independent status in relation to the depart-

mental structure would be preserved, while at the same time
the number of direct managerial contacts with the chief
executive would be minimized.

As might be expected, this proposal also has encountered
vigorous opposition. A major difficulty inherent in this form
of organization appears to be the fact that the head of the
executive office, whether he be officially designated Secretary
or Under Secretary, would immediately attain a position of
influence in the administration second only to that of the
chief executive himself. Through his control over the budgetary, personnel, organizational, and planning activities of
the administration, the Secretary would be in a position to
"interpret" the broad course of executive policy, if not to
decide that policy himself.

The wisdom of such a development, so it is argued, may
well be doubted. The critics further contend that the exercise of the ultimate power of administrative direction is and
should remain the exclusive prerogative of the chief executive. The exercise of this power by a subordinate would
almost inevitably result in a concentration of authority without a commensurate development of responsibility. The responsibility for the administration of each department would
still rest upon the department heads subject to the direction
of the chief executive; the actual power to administer the
departments would, in certain particulars at least, be subject to limitations imposed by the *de facto* head of the executive department whether he were called Secretary or Under
Secretary—frequently without the knowledge of the chief
executive.

The result, for an indefinite period of time at any rate,
might well be uncertainty as to the lines of authority and a
considerable measure of administrative confusion. Orders
received from the executive department would be "checked
back to the White House" to discover whether the chief

executive had been consulted in connection with this particular or that. The argument previously addressed to the Secretary of the executive department would be reiterated to the chief executive. An inevitable consequence would be administrative delay, the reversal of certain decisions, and confusion. Moreover, if one can forecast the future on the basis of the past, there would be a considerable degree of "ganging up" on the part of the department heads against the "assistant President" with a consequent diminution in the operating efficiency of each of these over-all agencies.

The creation of such an executive department, moreover, would, in the opinion of its opponents, erect a still further barrier between the Treasury and those agencies of over-all management which are essentially fiscal in their character. The fact that the Budget Bureau was formerly in, though not of, the Treasury, enabled the two units to escape no little confusion in their operation.[2] The assignment of the Budget Bureau to the position of an independent agency in the Executive office in 1939 terminates the intimacy of the former relationship and may well necessitate a tremendous duplication both of records and personnel. It also remains to be seen whether the newly created division of administrative management of the Budget Bureau will work as effectively now that the Bureau has been divorced from direct Treasury contacts as it otherwise might.

In the opinion of these dissenters, legitimate doubt may likewise arise as to the desirability of including the service agencies—printing, procurement, library, and archives—in an essentially managerial and planning unit. Whether such inclusion would be conducive to the development of the

[2] This is, of course, a sheer assertion for which no documentary evidence has ever been advanced, and the fact that no great confusion has arisen since the two units were separated casts grave doubts upon its accuracy.

most desirable attitude on the part of these units toward the departments they are designed to serve is, it is urged, highly controversial. For better or for worse, the managerial function is traditionally regarded as a superior function, carrying with it the right to issue orders wherever necessary. There is, therefore, little or nothing in common between the managerial and the service units. The latter exist to aid and facilitate the departments in the accomplishment of their appointed tasks. They are, as their name indicates, service agencies, not managerial. If, by chance, they took on the attitude of their managerial confreres, the result would be detrimental to their service functions.

Thus it becomes apparent that this second proposal relative to the most advantageous allocation of the service, managerial and planning agencies is no less controversial than is the first.

Certain of the disadvantages which seemingly are inherent in the two proposals just discussed could, so it is urged, be obviated by a third method of organization—the transfer of these various service, managerial, and planning units to the Department of the Treasury, thus transforming it from a purely fiscal into a general managerial agency. This is, of course, the development which has taken place in Great Britain. Such a form of administrative organization makes possible, so the argument runs, a coördination of the diverse and overlapping activities of both the Bureau of the Budget and the Treasury and in so doing should minimize an unnecessary duplication of records and of personnel. Moreover, it should greatly facilitate the solution of those problems—centering for the most part in classification and salary schedules—which the Civil Service Commission, the Bureau of the Budget and the Treasury have in common. These problems, it should be noted incidentally, constantly recur; they arise not only in connection with each new unit of government created, but with any and every alteration of the career service involving an interdepartmental transfer. The increased intimacy between the personnel agency and the Treasury which the allocation of these various managerial units to the fiscal department would bring about, would, incidentally, be exceedingly advantageous, not so much because it would enable the Treasury to exert an influence for economy upon the personnel unit, but for the very opposite reason; it would enable the Civil Service Commission to educate the Treasury officials about various aspects of the personnel problem, and in so doing, it might well drive home the realization that very frequently the quest for true economy dictates an increase rather than a decrease in personnel expenditures. Furthermore, Treasury support of personnel recommendations might very well enhance the prestige of such proposals, and in so doing increase the probability of their legislative enactment.

In similar fashion the work of the division of administrative reorganization might likewise be facilitated by its inclusion in the fiscal department. Its activities, as has already been pointed out, will inevitably impinge upon the work not only of the Budget Bureau and the Civil Service Commission, but also upon that of the Treasury itself. The latter could, perhaps, be avoided if the duplication of the Budget Bureau and the Treasury records were complete. Such, however, will in all probability not be the case. If these latter units continue their independent existence, it can be taken for granted that an effort will be made to minimize duplication. The result will be that the division of administrative reorganization will be compelled to turn to both the Treasury and the Budget Bureau for the data upon which to base its analysis; and, as such data will not be collected with an eye to its later utilization by this division, it may be entirely inadequate. On the other hand, the integration of these managerial units with the Treasury should result, so the argument goes, not only in increased efficiency in the assembling of data from the departments, but, what is more, in a greater degree of collaboration between the division of administrative reorganization and the other managerial agencies and the Treasury itself.[3]

No less intimately related to the Treasury are the activities of the planning agency. Any significant planning which may be undertaken will almost inevitably have a financial aspect. And just as it is desirable to keep the pure scientist in the government service in close contact with the problems encountered by the field services, so is it imperative that the planners be compelled to give due consideration to the financial aspects of the problems with which they are dealing. Thus, although a proposed hydroelectric development of the river basins of the United States may be highly desirable from the point of view of future generations, the financial burden imposed by any such development upon the generation now living deserves serious consideration. Similarly, although six rooms, a bath, and an oil-burning furnace may be the ideal housing condition to which the submerged fifth of the population should be elevated, any proposal to attain this ideal through the use of government credit should certainly be subjected to thorough analysis by the Treasury not merely from the point of view of the possible impairment of the government's credit, but also from the point of view of its effect upon the tax base of the states and munici-

[3] The decision of the present administration to integrate the division of administrative reorganization or management with the Budget Bureau minimizes somewhat the difficulties which would have been inevitable had the former unit been given an independent status. It does not, however, solve the problem of the relation of these two agencies with the Treasury.

palities. The allocation of the planning agency to the Treasury should be conducive to such analyses.

The case for the allocation of the service agencies to the fiscal departments is by no means as strong, yet even here the proponents of this mode of organization insist that its advantages outweigh its drawbacks. In their opinion, despite the multiplicity of nonfiscal functions customarily carried on by the procurement division, the fact that most of its activities have a fiscal as well as a nonfiscal character justifies its inclusion in the Treasury. Similarly, as long as the engraving and printing of paper money and government bonds remains a Treasury function (and the necessities for minimizing the possibilities of forgery seem to dictate that it shall so remain) it appears to be self-evident that the maintenance of an independent printing establishment elsewhere necessarily means a duplication of both personnel and equipment, which could certainly be minimized if not eliminated if the function were completely centralized under Treasury auspices.

Such being the case, it seems obvious to the exponents of this thesis that the allocation of these various service, managerial, and staff agencies to the Department of the Treasury would *ipso facto* mean, not only the correlation of their mutually interrelated activities but also the coördination of these activities with those of the Treasury itself. Moreover, in contrast to the situation which would exist if these agencies were given an independent status, such an integration would radically reduce the managerial burden upon the chief executive.

Conclusive as this line of reasoning may appear, it also has given rise to biting criticism. In the first place, the proponents of the English mode of organization have, in the opinion of their critics, greatly oversimplified the arguments. The types of printing carried on by the Bureau of Engraving and the Printing Office, for example, clearly differ so radically that any proposal to consolidate the work of these two units is simply absurd. The work of the Bureau of Engraving is so vitally connected with the integrity of the monetary system of the country that extraordinary care must clearly be taken not merely with the selection of its personnel but also with the continued supervision thereof. To apply the same care to the selection and supervision of the employees of the United States Printing Office generally would be an unnecessary expenditure both of time and money. If the two units were subordinated to the Treasury, it is almost self-evident that it would be necessary to continue their distinct and separate existences. The sum total result consequently would be the allocation to the Treasury of a nonfiscal agency, the activities of which would have no more connection with the Treasury than they would with any other department, and a consequent increase in the criticism and jealousy now existing.

Similarly, as the critics of the proposal see the situation, the present inclusion in the Treasury of a purchasing division, bereft though that division now is of its public works aspects, may well be challenged. In one sense, it is true, the Procurement Division may be thought of as a fiscal agency, but in one sense only. It is a spending agency. And in this respect it differs only slightly from the Departments of War, State, Agriculture, or any one of a multiplicity of administrative units. Its position in the Treasury is rendered a little more justifiable than would be the inclusion of any administrative unit picked at random by virtue of the fact that it is nonfunctional in character. Nevertheless, the *raison d'être* of the Procurement Division's present departmental allocation is primarily that of expediency. The charges of departmental favoritism which occasionally arise in connection with its administration suggest that the reasons of

expediency which have dictated its inclusion in the Treasury
are rather controversial.

Aside from the irrelevance of the activities of the various
and sundry service agencies to the main objective of the
Treasury Department's work, and the consequent neglect
such irrelevance frequently produces, an even more serious
disadvantage might result from the inclusion of these agencies in a managerial department, a disadvantage already referred to—the possibility that the essentially service agencies might take on the color and develop the attitude of the
managerial units. In view of the fact that these administrative units are not ends in themselves but services designed
to facilitate the work of the different departments, any
such coloration would go a long way toward defeating the
very purposes for which these agencies have been instituted.

No less untenable, in the eyes of the critics of the proposal, is the reasoning advanced above as to the advantages
of incorporating the planning and managerial agencies in the
Treasury.

Whatever may be said about the proper location of such
general managerial agencies as the Budget Bureau, the
place of an over-all planning agency in administration is
less open to differences of opinion. By definition, a planning
agency's function is to analyze the problems of the federal
government and the nation from a long-time, over-all point
of view, for the purpose of helping the chief executive
formulate both his executive orders and his recommendations to the legislature. The work of a planning agency, in
consequence, must cover not only the activities of all the
existing agencies of the federal government, but the whole
complex of our political, economic and social life as well.

Its work is to be differentiated from that of the departments and the independent administrative agencies in two
ways. In the first place, its sole function is that of recom-

mendation and suggestion. It is in no way an administrative or managerial unit. Any suggestions it may make, any plans it may propose, must of necessity be transmitted to the chief executive for such use as he may see fit to make of them. The responsibility for their utilization or nonutilization rests squarely upon the chief executive. Aside, perhaps, from the function of fuller exposition, the planning agency's connection with its recommendations ceases upon their transmission to the chief executive. The execution of such plans as may be approved by him rests exclusively upon the managerial and administrative units.

In the second place, the problems with which such an over-all planning agency deals, will, for the most part, be superdepartmental in scope: they will be either of such a character as to require interdepartmental planning, or entirely beyond the jurisdiction of the existing administrative agencies. In any event the function of such a planning agency will not be a mere duplication of the efforts of a particular department or other administrative unit in given fields.

Thus, although it is true that the work of the planning agency will impinge upon the activities of the Treasury, it will similarly impinge upon the activities of every other administrative unit in the entire governmental organization. There is, in the opinion of the critics of the English mode of organization, therefore, little more reason for assigning it to the Treasury than there is for allocating it to any other department. The chief function of a planning agency, it should be emphasized again, is working out the solution of problems, whether these problems are in the realm of water power, housing, welfare, or what not. The solution of these problems will ordinarily call for the expenditure of considerable sums of money. To place the planning agency in an administrative department which historically at least has had a "penny pinching" tradition, might easily lead to a stifling of imagination and ideas. Long-range planning for economic and social ends might well be discouraged by Treasury officials because of the financial exigencies of the moment. In such an atmosphere the very concept of planning might die at birth.

The fact that the allocation of the various and sundry staff, service, and managerial units to the Treasury would to some extent transform it from a fiscal to a managerial agency in no way minimizes the force of this reasoning. To some degree, it enhances it. For the subordination of the planning agency to a managerially minded Treasury might well result in overburdening the planning agency with requests for plans and blueprints of administrative procedures designed to effect petty economies to such an extent that the major, more fundamental problems to which theoretically the staff agency should be devoting its attention might well be crowded out. In the minds of the Treasury officials such a development would probably be looked upon as the proper subordination of the esoteric impulses of the planning agency to more practical considerations. Moreover, the increased intimacy between the staff and the managerial agencies which would probably develop as a result of their allocation to a single department might, as has already been suggested, undermine the very *raison d'être* of the planning agencies, and convert them into handmaidens for those agencies interested in the exigencies of the moment. In other words, the integration of the planning agencies with a managerially minded Treasury might easily be conducive, so these analysts believe, to the loss of their most vital characteristics, without which the reason for their continued existence is, for the most part, destroyed.

A much more powerful argument can be advanced for the inclusion of the managerial units in the Treasury, yet even here, too, in the opinion of the opponents of the proposal, the reasoning is seriously defective. For example, despite the obvious fact that that phase of personnel management concerned with salary schedules and the like is distinctly fiscal in character, the bulk of the work of the Civil Service Commission is of quite a different nature. It is largely concerned with the problems of "recruitment, examination and placement; probation; transfer and promotion; discipline; retirement; the establishment of personnel records; hours of duty; holidays and sick leaves; health, safety and welfare," to list only a few items. The allocation of the personnel agency to the Treasury Department, consequently, might easily result in the subordination of the more important nonfiscal aspects of the personnel agency's work to the fiscal, if for no other reason than that the Treasury would, in all probability, be less interested in the nonfiscal aspect of the work. Moreover, a Treasury situs might well subordinate the personnel agency to such penny-pinching traditions as might prevail in the fiscal department, and cause the agency to conceive of its task as primarily the hiring of administrative personnel as cheaply as possible, while ignoring other facets of its problem.

From a strictly fiscal point of view, the integration of the Bureau of the Budget and the Treasury might well be advantageous. There is, however, one paramount consideration applicable alike to the Budget Bureau, the personnel agency, and the division of administrative organization, which should receive further emphasis; it is the fact that the inclusion in the Treasury of any or all of the managerial agencies aforementioned would in some measure convert the Department from a purely fiscal administrative unit into a managerial one; and in so doing would elevate the Secretary of the Treasury from his position as the mere head of a department to one of preëminence and power over his cabinet associates. His authority would encompass not merely the activities of his own department but vital aspects of the work of other departments as well. Indeed, in view of the pressure of political and ceremonial matters upon the time of the chief executive, the result might well be the delegation to the Secretary of Treasury of practically unsupervised powers of administrative management. He might become, in fact if not in name, the assistant or deputy President.

This immediately raises a question discussed earlier in connection with the possible creation of an executive department: Would such a development be wise? The line of reasoning advanced by the critics of the proposal is similar in all essentials to that advanced previously. The importance of the subject alone justifies its reiteration.

The concentration of these tremendous managerial powers in the hands of a financially minded Secretary of Treasury might, the critics of the proposal maintain, lead to Treasury sabotage. Under certain administrations at least economy rather than the solution of particular problems is one of the major objectives of the Treasury. Under these circumstances, it is asserted, the full force of these various and sundry managerial powers might be turned in this direction to the detriment of other activities. Moreover, any such enhancement of the powers of the Secretary of the Treasury would unquestionably lead to envy and jealousy on the part of other cabinet officers, with a consequent disruption of administration in those matters in which interdepartmental coöperation is vital.

Much more fundamental, in the opinion of the dissenters, is the fact that such a delegation of authority might, to some degree at least, as was suggested earlier in the chapter, distort or pervert one of the fundamental principles of our constitutional organization. Although, in a measure, a national election may be said to be a choice between parties, to a considerable degree at least it is a choice between individual candidates. And, under the presidential system, it is the chief executive, not his Secretary of the Treasury, who is elected. In the hands of the chief executive is vested by constitutional provision the executive authority of the government. Obviously this does not mean that the chief executive cannot or should not delegate ministerial functions to his chief subordinates. It does mean, however, that the full responsibility for the entire administration of that government rests with him. A corollary of this is that the chief executive should retain under his own immediate direction and control the implementation necessary to his managerial functions. The budget bureau, the division of efficiency, the personnel and staff agencies are all essentially planning and managerial units. The subordination of these agencies to the Secretary of the Treasury or any other department head, consequently, would mean a partial abdication on the part of the chief executive of the very powers he was elected to exercise, and as such constitutes at least a partial frustration of the desires of the electorate. The fact that the Secretary of the Treasury holds office at the will of the chief executive is not a complete refutation of this line of reasoning. For, although presumably the chief executive will be able to obtain from these managerial units such information as he may desire, their reports will be made through the medium of their departmental superior. Under these circumstances, consequently, the Secretary of Treasury can and probably would exercise large discretion in conveying information to the office of the chief executive. And, in so doing, he would exercise a discretion which constitutionally belongs to the chief executive alone.[4]

[4] The President of the United States could, of course, dismiss the Secretary of Treasury whenever he wished, but he would be likely to do

The question arises, Does not this same line of reasoning apply to the British system? Obviously not, for the chief executive of Great Britain is the Cabinet not the Prime Minister. The responsibility is collegiate not individual. In consequence, the actions of the Treasury are subject to review and redirection by the heads of the various departments who, in the sense we have been using the term, are subject to Treasury control. By virtue of this fact the action of the British Treasury is at all times subject to a check which would be nonexistent under American conditions if the Treasury were transformed from a fiscal to a managerial agency.

A fourth possible method of organization remains to be explored: the consideration of each of these over-all agencies individually, and the allocation of each to that position in the administrative structure most suited to its own peculiar function. Thus certain of these units might be assigned to the Treasury; others, to the Office of the Chief Executive; while the remaining units might be granted an autonomous status or given a place within the departmental structure as the conveniences of efficient administration may suggest.

Under these circumstances it seems apparent to certain analysts that the Bureau of the Budget, the over-all agency possessing the most distinctly fiscal characteristics, should *ipso facto* be transferred to the Treasury. This would, as was pointed out, obviate the duplication of records and of personnel that complete separation makes probable, and it would also encourage coördination of the activities of these two administrative units, which are so essentially fiscal in character.

so in connection with some crisis rather than because of disagreement over the day-to-day detail of administration.

To others, however, this is far from self-evident. The fact that such a procedure would place in the hands of the Sceretary of Treasury managerial and policy-determining powers far transcending the boundaries of his own department, thereby giving rise to interdepartmental jealousies and frictions, completely offsets, in their opinion, any advantages which might be inherent in the integration of this agency with the Treasury. The further fact that such an arrangement would, as was elaborated earlier, deprive the chief executive of personal direction and control of the most important instrumentality of over-all supervision in the administration, and by so doing would not merely invade the prerogatives conferred upon him by the Constitution but would also, to a limited degree at least, pervert the spirit and purpose of democratic organization, completes the refutation of the proposal.

An alternative possibility which has the support of one wing of these dissenting analysts is the restoration of the relationship which existed between the Bureau of the Budget and the Treasury prior to the Reorganization Plan of 1939, i.e., the Bureau of the Budget might be "in the Treasury but not of it." This relationship was so characterized, it will be recalled, because the head of the Bureau of the Budget was appointed by the President by and with the consent of the Senate and was removable by him alone. Thus the head of the Bureau was in no way subject to the orders of the Treasury. Instead, he had at all times the right to report directly to the chief executive rather than through the medium of the Secretary of the Treasury. Others among the dissenters favor the assignment of the Budget Bureau to an independent position in the administrative structure subordinate only to the chief executive himself. The line of reasoning in support of this allocation has already been developed and need not be reiterated here. In any event, it is apparent that the mere enunciation of the principle that each of the over-all agencies should be considered individually and allocated to that position in the administrative structure most suited to its needs does not automatically solve the problem.

Much less controversial than the proper situs of the Budget Bureau in the administrative structure, in so far as these analysts are concerned, is the proper location of the personnel agency. Despite the fact that certain aspects of this unit's activities are fiscal in character, the bulk of its work lies in other fields. The inclusion of this agency under the Treasury Department, therefore, would in their opinion have only the advantage of providing a superior officer to adjudicate any differences which might arise between it and the other administrative units included in the Treasury. This, in view of the enormous number of contacts between this agency and the other units of administration, is, of course, of negligible importance. Much more significant is the fact that the subordination of this agency to the Secretary of the Treasury might lead to the neglect of the non-fiscal aspects of its work. Finally, as these students of the subject see it, the allocation of the personnel agency to the Treasury would at one and the same time enhance the power and prestige of the Secretary of the Treasury and deprive the chief executive of a further immediate instrumentality of administrative supervision and control— a deprivation which, as was indicated earlier, would in fact if not in legal theory infringe upon his constitutional prerogatives and, to some extent at least, undermine the basic principles of democratic organization.

It would be possible, of course, to incorporate the personnel agency in the Treasury upon the basis previously occupied by the Bureau of the Budget. But, even under these circumstances, whether the influence of the Treasury would be good or ill would, in their opinion, remain enigmatical. If the Bureau of the Budget itself is not included in the Treasury, whatever validity the arguments for including the personnel agency in the fiscal department may have had is reduced to zero. The general conclusion to which this line of analysis leads is that while the personnel agency might conceivably be given a place "in but not of the Treasury," if such a status is assigned to the Bureau of the Budget, the preponderance of reasoning suggests that it be assigned an autonomous position in the administrative structure, subordinate only to the chief executive.

So intimately related to the activities of the Bureau of the Budget and the personnel agency, in the opinion of these analysts, is the work of the division of administrative organization that the proper place for this unit is almost automatically determined by the decisions taken in connection with the other two. If both are located in the Department of the Treasury, the division of administrative organization would almost necessarily be assigned the same situs. Here, too, however, the questions recur: Would it be wise to subordinate a partially nonfiscal agency to the control of a fiscally minded Secretary of the Treasury? Should the managerial powers which are constitutionally vested in the chief executive be delegated, in fact if not in constitutional theory, to a mere department head? The general reaction to these questions of the analysts who subscribe to this fourth concept of organization has already been indicated.

In connection with the division of administrative organization, however, a further question arises: Should independent status be given a unit as small as this agency is likely to be for a good many years to come? Should it not rather be incorporated in some thoroughly established administrative organization?

The chief advantage to be attained by granting an autonomous position to this agency is the fact that such a mode of organization would give it complete liberty in the pursuit of its investigations. It should be able, consequently, to devote itself to major problems of reorganization as well as to minor reforms of administrative processes. Such might not be the case if it were completely subordinate to some other administrative agency, whether the Treasury or the Bureau of the Budget. Under the latter condition it is not only conceivable, but perhaps probable, that in the course of time its activities will more and more be directed to the improvement of these day-to-day minutiae of administration which although exceedingly important do not constitute the whole problem. Moreover, if one can judge the future by the past, there will always be the tendency on the part of a large organization to sacrifice its subsidiaries in the occasional drives for petty economy instituted by Congress.

The disadvantage of granting such a small unit an independent status is that it will get lost in the vortex of administration. Relatively unimportant in the day-by-day conduct of administration, it will neither receive that coöperation from the other administrative units which is important if it is to perform its task effectively, nor will it have sufficient prestige to give its recommendations the weight which will be necessary if they are to be translated into administrative action. Both of these disadvantages could be obviated if the division of administrative organization were incorporated in some larger well-established over-all unit. The analysts suggest that the obvious unit with which the division of administrative organization might be integrated is the Bureau of the Budget. To an extent that is true of no other administrative agency; the work of the Bureau of the Budget complements that of the division of administrative organization. The Bureau of the Budget occupies a strategic position in consequence of which the other administrative units are likely to be both willing and eager to coöperate. Moreover, because of its control over the purse strings, limited though that may be, its suggestions are likely to be treated with the greatest respect and to receive the fullest consideration.

Quite different in its character from these managerial agencies is the planning unit. It has, or should have, as has already been indicated, an over-all, long-range point of view, combined with a complete renunciation of managerial aspirations. Its *forte* is that of suggestion and recommendation. Its inclusion in the Treasury, in the opinion of most of those who espouse this fourth pattern of organization, would in no way enhance its efficiency. Instead, it might narrow the breadth and depth of its thinking, and transform it into an adjunct of the service and managerial agencies. Moreover, if inclusion within the Treasury Department precluded direct reporting to the chief executive, the result of such an allocation would be the delegation to the Secretary of the Treasury of discretionary power which probably belongs to the chief executive himself. On the other hand, if this unit were incorporated in the Treasury upon the same basis as that formerly occupied by the Bureau of the Budget, not even a reduction of the number of administrative pressures upon the chief executive would result. In consequence, there would appear to be little or no gain to be secured by such a procedure. The conclusion seems inescapable: the planning agency may well be given an autonomous position in the administrative structure subject only to the chief executive himself.

A number of other over-all agencies remain to be discussed: the Library of Congress, the National Archives, the Government Printing Office and the Procurement Division. Designed to serve the executive department, Congress, and the general public, it is quite apparent that no particular advantage would be attained by allocating to the Treasury, or for that matter to any other department, either the Congressional Library or the National Archives. A completely autonomous position for these agencies can, consequently, be justified. In like fashion there appears to these analysts to be little or no reason for including the Government Printing Office in the departmental structure. The apparent reasons for its allocation to the Treasury are, as has already been pointed out, fallacious. Designed to serve both Congress and the departments, the allocation of this unit to the Treasury or any other department would only complicate the administrative process, and might conceivably be conducive to the charge, if not the fact, of departmental favoritism.

The problem of the Procurement Division is more complicated. Its public-works activities certainly had no place in the Treasury Department and should have been transferred to a public-works unit long ago, as they finally were by the Reorganization Plan of April 25, 1939. Its other activities—purchasing, leasing, coördinating, transport, etc.—fall in a different category, and may to some extent impinge upon the work of the division of administrative organization, but only to a very limited degree. If, consequently, it should appear desirable for reasons of administrative convenience to minimize the number of independent autonomous units, and if the Bureau of the Budget, the division of administrative organization, and the rest are allotted to the Treasury, the nonconstruction aspects of the Procurement Division might in the eyes of these analysts be maintained in the Treasury upon the same basis. If, however, the Bureau of the Budget, and the other managerial agencies are allocated to an independent position subordinate only to the chief executive, the case for its retention in the Treasury is much weakened. Under these circumstances, however, the Procurement Division, shorn of its construction aspects, might still remain in the Treasury, merely as a matter of convenience.

As a result of the preceding discussion it should be apparent that in still another aspect of the field of administration the study of the subject has as yet failed to evolve any universally accepted scientific principles capable of automatic application. Instead, a number of divergent concepts are seemingly contending for acceptance.

Actually the fundamental cleavage between these concepts turns upon the desired characteristics of the chief executive and his relation to the legislative body. At the one extreme are those who subscribe to the Hamiltonian concept that the federal executive should be endowed with powers commensurate with the responsibilities constitutionally and traditionally imposed upon him—an executive capable of both planning and executing the policies of the nation. A logical corollary of this postulate is the belief of these analysts that the service, managerial, and planning agencies should be located in the White House subject to the personal direction and control of the chief executive. At the other extreme are those who fear the possibility of Caesarism, who prefer the compromise policies of representative government to the more unified and potentially more internally consistent policies of a powerful chief executive. No less logically deduced from their premises is the desire of these analysts to grant the several service, managerial, and planning agencies an autonomous position in the administrative structure subject only to the direction of the statutes. With this status, they assert, the over-all agencies will be under a greater degree of congressional control than would otherwise be the case. Between these two extremes lie any number of variations in fundamental attitude. From these flow an equal variety of methods of organization.

In the final analysis, therefore, the choice of the particular manner in which the service, managerial, and planning agencies will be distributed throughout the administrative structure will rest not upon the ratiocinations of the experts, but upon the fundamental postulates or predelictions of those who make the ultimate decision.

INFORMAL CONTROLS

Each of the· instrumentalities of interdepartmental organization we have been discussing thus far is designed to deal with activities and problems which constantly recur. Inevitably in the operation of the vast administrative machinery of a modern government interdepartmental problems will arise which do not recur or occur only intermittently and which cannot be institutionalized. Some of these will relate to matters of public policy that can only be settled by the chief executive. Others will be of lesser importance, capable of being settled at the departmental level. Some will be concerned with broad questions of administrative policy; others will be so specialized that only the technicians can handle them; still others, no less important in their total consequence, will be small day-to-day items that can usually be settled by a telephone call or an exchange of letters.

The fact that these nonroutinized interdepartmental activities are subject to no single supervisory authority short of the chief executive himself—i.e., that they do not fall in the categories supervised by the various service and managerial agencies—will from time to time give rise to interdepartmental maladjustments; these, if not overcome, will be conducive to gross inefficiency, a duplication of personnel, an overlapping of activities, inadequate planning, lack of teamwork, and frequently a working at cross purposes.

Although open warfare between two or more departments is relatively rare in Washington, lack of coöperation is far from uncommon. Thus, as has already been indicated, the various financial units of the administration went their own ways for a short period of time, at any rate in connection

with the flotation of bond issues, with little or no consideration of the effect of their flotations upon the other financial
agencies of the government. Not until the passage of the
Social Security Act did the diverse agencies dealing with
public health make any serious effort to coördinate their
activities. The coolness between the various "consumer"
units scattered through the administration is a matter of
common knowledge. Rivalry and jealousy rather than mutual coöperation has marked the attitude of certain of the
housing units to each other.

In part these various situations have been due to faulty
departmentalization. In so far as this is true, a thoroughgoing departmental reorganization should go a long way
toward preventing their recurrence. In part it has been due
to ignorance of what was going on elsewhere in the government. In part it is due to lethargy. Interdepartmental coöperation inevitably means interference with administrative
routine. In part it is due to what, for want of a better phrase,
we have already referred to as bureaucratic imperialism:
the tendency upon the part of bureau chiefs and other subordinate administrators to strive to expand the scope of the
administrative unit or units under their direction.[5] This may

[5] In this aspect, the problem falls more largely in the field of personnel administration than it does in that of administrative organization. The two fields, however, are so intertwined that a slight digres-
sion is, perhaps, justifiable.

Stated in its simplest terms, the personnel problem involved may
be said to be the discovery of ways and means to sublimate bureaucratic ambitions into departmental and interdepartmental channels.
To this end the suggestion has been made that the civil service be
extended upward as well as downward and outward. The mere existence
of superior posts to which the administrative personnel may aspire,
will, so it is urged (and quite soundly), stimulate the subordinate administrators to think in departmental rather than bureaucratic terms.
Similarly it is urged: the creation of a system of interdepartmental
promotion with transfers to and from the various over-all agencies

be due to the distorted perspective of a bureau chief so immersed in the work of his particular administrative unit that all other things appear subsidiary to it. Or it may be due to an unbalanced sense of confidence in his own organization and a distrust of all others, with the concomitant feeling that his particular administrative unit is best equipped to handle all problems related to its field. Alternatively this bureaucratic imperialism may simply be a variation of the drive for power characteristic of many administrators. Or finally, it may merely be ambition for the larger financial reward in the administration of a large sized unit.

Whatever the cause, the result is the same, failure to coördinate properly the activities of the various administrative units concerned: duplication of personnel and frequently of material, inadequate planning, ineffective teamwork, and at times crossed purposes.

Inevitably the question arises: Should the solution of these intermittent interdepartmental difficulties be left to the common sense and initiative of the administrators in charge of the several units? Or should an effort be made to institutionalize a procedure which will ensure their more adequate handling? No less important is a second question: Can such a procedure be devised?

At the present time in Washington, tne endeavor to integrate these various interdepartmental activities takes place for the most part across the desk of the chief executive, in the Cabinet, by means of *ad hoc* interdepartmental committees and through the medium of informal conferences, exchanges of letters and telephone calls.

will be conducive to a degree of interdepartmental or over-all thinking at present almost nonexistent.

Moreover, the mere appointment of the more competent and frequently more aggressive subordinate officials to higher administrative posts will in and of itself contribute greatly to the minimization of bureaucratic imperialism.

It seems fairly obvious that a more adequate implementation of the Office of the Chief Executive should result not only in increased efficiency on the part of the chief executive in this particular, but should revitalize the Cabinet as an instrument of interdepartmental coördination. An extended discussion of these possibilities, however, lies outside the scope of this study.

In any event it seems very probable that the bulk of the interdepartmental relationships will continue to operate at the departmental level, and that the techniques most commonly used in their solution will continue to be those which have been utilized in the past—interdepartmental committees, informal conferences, telephone calls and the exchange of letters.

Of these, the most important from the point of view of organization at least, are the *ad hoc* interdepartmental committees. At the moment these committees receive their authority from three principal sources: Congress, the Chief Executive and the heads of the various departments. They usually arise out of a concrete situation, and begin with a discussion between the technicians or bureau chiefs most directly affected. Occasionally the initial conferences may be stimulated by someone outside the administration entirely. In any case, these initial proceedings may eventuate in further discussions involving the heads of the departments most vitally concerned, the chief executive, or even members of congressional committees and Congress itself.

Theoretically, there is a difference in the status of the interdepartmental committees resting on presidential or congressional authorization and those which are set up by mutual agreement between the departments concerned. The mere fact that the interdepartmental committees set up on the first of these bases report directly to the President or to Congress should be conducive to an over-all point of view in the approach to the problems assigned to them; whereas in the second case the members of these committees may quite logically look upon themselves as ambassadors from their respective departments.

In reality, however, no such differentiation can be made. The relative absence of either executive or legislative supervision over the committees resting on these respective authorizations reduces them in fact to the same level as all other interdepartmental committees. In a recently published monograph on the problem of interdepartmental committees in the national administration, Mary Trackett Reynolds concludes that the general effectiveness of all interdepartmental committees would be greatly improved if the lines of responsibility were more clearly drawn, whether to the head of the department primarily interested or to a Presidential secretariat. In consequence, if her conclusions are sound, and the evidence suggests that they are, the problem of interdepartmental integration through the medium of interdepartmental committees is in large measure a subsidiary aspect of the problem of executive implementation.[6]

No less important, than these institutional mechanisms for the attainment of interdepartmental integration, however, is the integration attainable through the dominance of particular ideals or policies. In his survey of American political institutions a little over a hundred years ago, Alexis de Tocqueville came to the conclusion that the equality of wealth and the manners of the country contributed more to the maintenance of democracy in the United States than either the laws or the physical environment. In like fashion, the contemporary observer of British and continental administration will be impressed with the part played in their respective administrations by "the traditions of the service."

[6] M. T. Reynolds, *Interdepartmental Committee.* (New York, 1939.)

One of the great problems of American administration is the creation of an *esprit de corps* in the American public service similar to that which exists in the great administrative organizations of Europe. For the most part, however, the solution of this problem lies in the development of a proper personnel policy. And as such it lies beyond the bounds of this analysis.

VIII ✦ ✦

CONCLUSIONS

ON THE BASIS OF THE PRECEDING ANALYSIS IT SHOULD BE apparent that any intelligent decision as to the type of administrative organization best suited to the needs of the country depends not upon some simple formula but upon the studied consideration of a multitude of factors. Some of these are seemingly only remotely connected, if at all, with the process of administration; they are, nevertheless, of transcendent importance.

Does the existing organization of our economic life represent the final stage in the development of American agriculture and industry or are tremendous chemurgical and technological changes impending? Is our present military organization adequate to the exigencies of modern warfare or will it be necessary in the United States as it has been in Europe to gear all our resources into the military machine? In the light of recent events can we any longer depend upon the unstable equilibrium of the market to dictate our further economic development or has economic planning become imperative? What agency in the federal government is best equipped to undertake such planning? Does the history of the Presidency or of Congress cast any light upon the problem? Can the bureaucracy be safely entrusted with enhanced powers without at the same time being subjected to further control? In whose hands should this control be lodged?

These are but a few of the questions which must be answered before an intelligent discussion of the technical

aspects of administration can begin. It is obviously beyond
the purview of this book to make decisions in connection
with these or any questions of a similar character which
might be asked. One thing, however, is clear: the organization of administration turns in large measure upon the fundamental purposes to which it is to be dedicated.

At times, these fundamental purposes are clearly set
forth; more often, however, they are embodied in certain
underlying assumptions or presuppositions both as to the
purposes of the organization of administration and the nature of society which nowhere see the light of day in discussion and are, of course, the inarticulate and unrecognized
major premises to which Holmes called attention in his
famous dictum.

Fully conscious of the fact that all work in the field of
public administration must, of necessity, rest upon a body
of fundamental postulates, conscious also of the dangers
involved in operating upon unrecognized preconceptions and
prejudices, the pioneers in the field of public administration
early adopted the practice of setting forth their basic assumptions and presuppositions. They boldly assumed the
existence of a capitalistic democracy, popular government
through a representative assembly and elected officials, and
the perdurance of the conception that the purpose of administration is to serve the requirements of such a society
with the utmost efficiency and economy. They recognized
that both tradition and contemporary practice held the
President largely responsible for the success or failure of
his administration and proposed therefore a budget which
would place in his hands the formulation and presentation
of the financial policies of the government. They recognized
frankly that there were dangers inherent in the enhancement of the powers of the chief executive and suggested a
program of legislative reorganization to offset them. As they

saw it, such dangers as existed did so primarily because of
the lethargy, inefficiency, and incompetence of Congress. In
their opinion, these could easily be overcome any time the
representative assembly chose to put its own house in order.

In thus delineating their fundamental postulates and presuppositions these early pioneers in the field of public administration stand in striking contrast to many contemporary students of the subject, who all too often present
their proposals for administrative reorganization and reform
without seeming consciousness of the fact that they are operating upon a set of hypotheses, or, if they are, carefully
concealing the hypotheses to protect them from criticism
or attack.

Thus, in the current controversy over the position of the
independent regulatory agencies in the administrative structure and the desirability of additional over-all controls over
administrative regulation generally, nowhere has there been
set forth the assumptions and presuppositions upon which
the proponents of the several plans rest their arguments.
Although these fundamental postulates and preconceptions
can only be deduced in part, it seems reasonable to believe
that the members of the American Bar Association who were
responsible for the formulation of the Walter-Logan Bill
were impressed by the invasion of what they conceive to be
the sphere of private rights which has followed the flood of
regulatory legislation recently enacted. The framers of this
bill apparently believe that if this flood is not completely to
submerge the traditional privileges of American citizens,
radical action is imperative. Further, the members of the
President's Committee on Administrative Management quite
obviously believed in the desirability of broad social planning and, as a concomitant of this, in the necessity of delegating to the chief executive discretionary power adequate

to the execution of these plans. Despite a disclaimer from the proponents of the so-called revisionist plan, one cannot help suspecting that its authors are pretty well satisfied with the *status quo*. Whether this is true or not, the startling fact is that the authors of the plan are so unaware of the influence of fundamental postulates and presuppositions upon the processes of thought that they boldly assert that the revisionists' plan "rests upon no assumptions."

Another contemporary controversy which involves, in large measure, certain inarticulate major premises is that relating to the proper situs in the administrative structure of the several over-all agencies. As was indicated earlier, this conflict turns upon the type of chief executive the proponents of the various plans desire and upon the proper distribution of power between that executive and the Congress; nevertheless, reams have been written without in any way touching upon this fundamental issue.

The influence of these fundamental postulates, let me emphasize again, is not confined to the problem of the independent regulatory commissions or to the over-all agencies. Instead, it ramifies into every nook and cranny of the administration. To what extent should the departmental organization be based upon a hierarchical or military principle with the line of command descending from the chief executive to the Secretary, to the Under Secretary, the Assistant Secretaries, and so on, down to the lowliest subordinate in the departmental organization? How far should certain particular administrative subdivisions be granted what might be called operating autonomy? Under what circumstances and to what degree should the convenience of the clientele become paramount over the administrative efficiencies attainable through other forms of departmental organization?

Such questions might be multiplied *ad infinitum*. But in each case certain fundamental assumptions regarding the nature of man and the character of society will inevitably color the conclusion. And since these underlying concepts will differ radically from individual to individual and from time and place to time and place, the answers to these several questions will likewise differ radically. The desirability of granting operating autonomy to departmental subdivisions because of the quasi-legislative, quasi-judicial character of their work will not receive the same weight from those who believe in "centralized planning" as it will from the exponents of "individual liberty." The convenience of the civil population will hardly be as paramount in time of war even in a democracy as it is in the days of peace.

These basic judgments relative to the nature of man and the character of society exert a decisive influence upon all thinking in the field of administration, or for that matter, in the social sciences. In view of this fact, it seems almost self-evident that one of the first steps in any comprehensive treatment of the subject is to return to the practices of the pioneers in the field and set forth, in so far as it is possible, the fundamental postulates upon which all proposals for administrative reorganization rest. For until these postulates have been exposed to discussion and criticism and their full implications discovered and explored, opposing schools of thought will continue to "talk past one another," and an all-around discussion of the administrative superstructure resting on these preliminary postulates will be out of the question.

A second conclusion suggested by the preceding analysis is that there exists a tendency on the part of many of those who deal with administration to concentrate upon some particular aspect of the general field and to ignore or neglect its relations to the process of government as a whole.[1] This tendency appears not merely in a failure to set forth and examine fundamental postulates and presuppositions, but also in the concrete recommendations made for administrative reform.

Thus, to repeat an illustration previously used, the American Bar Association is quite obviously concerned with the protection of private rights against governmental regulation rather than with the whole problem of government and economy in a modern society. Nowhere in the briefs is there any indication that the Association has viewed the business of governmental regulation from the administrative side or seriously considered the administrative problems which would result from its proposals to reform the existing regulatory organization. Similarly the members and staff of the President's Committee on Administrative Management concentrated their attention on the problem of over-all management, although in fairness it should be said that they did not neglect entirely the necessity of exploring the probable effects of their recommendations upon the Congress and the courts. Nevertheless their explorations in this direction were relatively negligible in comparison to the amount of attention they gave to the subject of administrative organization under their immediate consideration. The Brookings Institution, likewise, to its credit, did not confine its investigations to the narrow field of reference which was set for it by the terms of its contract with the Congressional Committee, but it operated clearly upon its own assumptions.

Those who deal with administration generally do not look

[1] It is interesting to note that a large number of those who have not fallen in with this general tendency have come to the study of administration through other phases of the field of political science, e. g., political philosophy, politics, etc. By virtue of this fact they have had a background which has enabled them to note interrelations which are frequently overlooked by the specialist.

upon the study of that subject as requiring the study of government as a whole—much less as necessitating a broad consideration of the economic, social, and psychological characteristics of the society in which they are operating.

With the exception of Harvey Mansfield in his excellent monograph on the Comptroller's Office, no one, for example, has seriously studied the role of legislative criticism in the administrative process. Such studies as have been made by students of administration have, as far as I know, been without exception the other way around—the relation of the chief executive to the legislature.

This total neglect of the role of legislative participation in the process of administration is all the more startling in the light of certain lessons which apparently can be drawn from European history, not to mention the record of American experience. It seems highly probable, for example, that the decline of effective criticism both from the Roman Senate and Assembly may have had something to do with the decreased efficiency of the Roman bureaucracy which preceded the disintegration of the Empire of the Caesars. Some correlation may conceivably have existed between the lack of popular and legislative criticism and the corruption and inefficiency of the old Russian civil service. The fact that the transformation of the British administrative service from an aggregation of place men and plunderers into a service which has won the admiration of the world coincided with the extension of popular government may have some implications worth investigating. Even the extension of the Prussian bureaucracy from the handmaiden of a small agricultural state to the backbone of an Empire occurred concomitantly with the development of an organ of criticism, limited though it was, the Reichstag. Nor is the record wholly silent in the United States. From the administration of George Washington to that of Franklin Roosevelt, Congress has acted not merely as a policy-determining body but also as a participant in and critic of the administration. On the basis of available data, it is impossible to determine whether the existence of a vehicle for popular criticism is the indispensable element in the process of administration without which long-continued efficiency and honesty appear to be improbable; but there is more than negligible evidence indicating that such is the case.

From the point of view of the present discussion the significant thing is that students of administration have not taken the trouble to investigate the matter of legislative-administrative relations to the point which admits of practical conclusions. Nor have they paid much if any attention to ways and means by which legislative criticism might be made more informed and effective—whether through superior committee organization and procedure, an adaptation of the English question hour, the French Parliamentary Commissions, or some other device.

On the other hand, students of administration only rarely inquire into the probable effects of their proposals for administrative reform on political or social institutions. What effect will the increasing implementation of the power of the chief executive have upon the status and power of representative assemblies? Are we in the guise of administrative efficiency evolving a form of Caesarism? Nowhere—or only rarely—are such questions ever discussed by those who treat of administration.

These observations upon the tendency of students of administration to become engrossed with some particular aspects of administration and sometimes to constitute themselves apologists for the bureaucracy are not, needless to say, intended as reflections upon the excellent technical work which is going on in the United States. Instead they are designed to suggest breadth of vision as well as specialization as a prime prerequisite for the development of a more comprehensive science of administration.

In view of all the controversies considered in the preceding pages, it may be asked: Is not a science of administration a sheer impossibility? Does not the fact that much of the thinking in the field of administration must of necessity rest upon unverified, and in many cases unverifiable, postulates, i.e., value judgments, preclude such a development? This condition, it must be conceded, introduces numerous complications not to be found in the natural sciences. Nevertheless, as Hans Vaihinger has long since pointed out in *The Philosophy of "As If,"* even mathematics, that most exact of all sciences, rests upon a series of fictions. Not merely are curves subsumed under straight lines but the fundamental concepts of mathematics "space, or more precisely empty space, empty time, point, line, surface, or more precisely points without extension, lines without breadth, surfaces without depth, space without content"—are not merely fictions but contradictory fictions, and to the introduction of these fictions and the ingenious methods based upon them, mathematics owes its remarkable advance in modern times. But if remarkable progress has been made upon the foundation of consciously and unconsciously accepted and frequently contradictory fictions, "the frank acknowledgment of these fundamental contradictions has become absolutely essential for [further] mathematical progress."

Similarly the study of administration has also advanced upon the basis of half-truths and fictions and there is no reason to believe that further progress will not still be made. But a distinction should be noted between the hypotheses and fictions of science and the value judgments which so frequently underlie the conclusions of thought pertaining to administration. By definition an hypothesis is a tentative statement of fact which remains to be verified or discarded; fictions "are assumptions made with the full realization of the impossibility of the thing assumed, whether because it is internally contradictory, or because on external grounds it cannot constitute reality," and are also to be discarded when they are no longer useful. Value judgments, on the other hand, are assertions of opinion or alleged fact which have not been and frequently cannot be verified. Thus, thinking in the field of administration must proceed subject to the handicap of perpetually unverifiable assumptions. Although it seems highly probable that great strides may yet be made in those particular aspects of the field of administration in which the data can be reduced to measurable terms, nevertheless the student of public administration must be continuously on guard to recognize the character of the intellectual operations which he is conducting.

But has not sufficient progress already been made which would justify, even today, the characterization of the subject as a science?

The problem is to some extent one of terminology. If by science one means only an organized body of knowledge, then undoubtedly the field of administration is a science at the present moment. But so also are cookery, embalming, carpentry, and a multitude of other fields in connection with which a body of experience has been accumulated and recorded. In this sense the term is practically meaningless.

If, however, a science is understood to mean the existence of a body of organized knowledge on the basis of which it has been possible to found a number of completely verified general principles of universal application, then it must be admitted that the study of administration is far from deserving such a characterization. In view of the fact that its fundamental postulates are to a surprising degree a series of value judgments hidden away in inarticulate major premises, it is problematical at least whether administration ever will attain the status of a true science.

The danger of labeling "scientific" such findings as exist in the field of administration is that the use of this euphuism in general nomenclature is likely to lead to the use of similarly inaccurate words in subsidiary terminology. Broad generalizations are apt to be put forward as principles when in fact they are the most tentative of hypotheses or assumptions. Although such a procedure may be in no way catastrophic so far as the sophisticates are concerned, such loose terminology is very likely to contribute to loose thinking. Moreover, the use of such grandiose terminology, carrying, in certain instances, the implication of the possession of ultimate truths, may easily lead to a condition of rigor mortis in the study of administration similar to that which once characterized the study of political science.

In other words, it may accentuate and accelerate the all too human tendency to accept an existing body of postulates, presuppositions, and value judgments, and the generalizations alleged to be drawn therefrom, as eternal verities above the necessity of analysis or reappraisal—a tendency which has been strikingly revealed in the past, not only by the fabled discussion of the scholastics as to how many angels could dance upon the point of a needle but also by certain ratiocinations emanating from the social sciences.

No less important for the development and reputation of administration is the fact that terming this field of knowledge a science will inevitably lead to an attempt on the part of reformers who use its findings in practice to palm off on the public as "scientific" mere proposals which are in fact tentative conclusions, many of them mere deductions from inarticulate major premises. This is, of course, no reflection upon the activities of the practitioners in administrative installations. In most instances their recommendations are probably more realistic than the concepts of the politicians and pressure groups with which they have to contend. Nevertheless their recommendations should be considered on their merits and not cloaked behind unjustifiable claims of scientific omniscience.

Such being the case, it would seem wise for students of administration to restrain their desire for recognition as scientists and to concentrate their efforts upon a further development in their chosen field of study. Among the prerequisities for such an advance would appear to be: (1) a greater recognition of the connection between underlying assumptions or presuppositions and the character and quality of thinking in the field; (2) the development of some technique or process of thought which will bring these assumptions to light and subject them to analysis and criticism and, equally important, indicate the limitations of the superstructure of thought which can be erected upon them; (3) a greater realization of the necessity of taking into consideration all discernible relevancies rather than concentrating upon some particular aspect or phase of the subject to the total exclusion of others; (4) the avoidance of formulas too simple to encompass the pertinent facts; and (5) the development of a terminology in respect of all generalizations which will at one and the same time indicate the extent of their applicability and their limitations. In this fashion the study of administration may eventually come to merit the appellation to which it now aspires.

INDEX

Congress (*continued*)
independent regulatory agencies,
148, 149, 151, 164, 165; presidential programs forced through,
159, 164; inadequate control of
chief executive, 160, 162, 163;
use of vague terms, 174; implementation of control over executive and administration, 183, 184;
distribution of power between
executive and, 220, 230; legislative
reorganization proposed, 228; as
critic of administration, 234
Congressional Library, 187, 195, 198,
201, 218
Conservation, Department of (proposed), 105, 196
Control, span of: by chief executive, 39-44; by subordinates, 48
Coolidge, Calvin, 73
Coördination, exigency of decentralization and, 19-38; coöperation
between local units of government, 25 ff.; by negotiation, 27;
difficulty inherent in functional
devolution, 32; departmentalization, a method of, 36 f.; French
attempt to superimpose ministers
of, 44, 87; arguments for fewer
and larger departments rests on
degree of, attained, 45, 47; lack
of, between departments, 46,
47, 221; applicable to units engaged in related activities, 48;
necessity for interdepartmental
consultation and action, 60;
v. operating autonomy in departmentalization, 74-90; military, 75, 76, 99, 116; in holding-
company mode of organization,
76, 85; burden imposed upon
chief executive by process departments, 115; in departments integrated upon basis of clientele, 125,
129; upon basis of place, or territory, 136
Coördinator of Transportation, 101
Corporations, government-owned, 79

Corps of Engineers, 49, 60, 82, 140
Council of State Governments, 26
County governments, 30
Court of Appeals for Administra-
tion, 179, 184
Courts, plan to lodge control of in-
dependent regulatory agencies in,
168-73, 174 f., 176
Criticism of administration, 43 f.,
233 f.
Customs, Bureau of, 104

Decentralization, exigency of coordination and, 19-38; geographic,
of political institutions, 20-29;
advantages and defects, 24 f., 27;
older forms breaking down, 28;
functional devolution, 29-35; departmentalization, 35-38; exact
compromise between advantages
of centralization and, 135
Delay, as a result of departmental
size, 58, 64
Democratic society, existence assumed, 12, 14, 228
Departmentalization, process of,
35-38; as a principle of administration, 37; problems, 38; quantitative considerations, 39-73; chief
executive's span of control the
fundamental postulate, 39-44;
number of departments in various countries, 40; criticism, 43 f.,
233 f.; influence and effect of
various patterns, 45; arguments
for fewer and larger departments,
45-58, 69; for more and smaller
ones, 58-69, 70; summarized, 69-
73; variation in amount of routine or quantitatively measurable
activity, 71; factors of routine
operation and judgment, 72; coordination versus operating autonomy in, 74-90; application of
holding-company principle to government, 77; considerations which
enter into the construction of a
department, 91-146; functional

Justice, Department of, 112, 114, 172*n*

Labor, Department of, 47, 51, 64, 65, 67, 98, 102, 124, 131; Children's Bureau, 46, 65, 123, 127, 128, 130; independence, 51, 66, 68
Labor, Division of, in a Department of Social Affairs, 66
Labor Relations . . . , *see* National Labor Relations . . .
Labor Statistics, Bureau of, 47
Land Office, 46
Land Utilization, Department of (proposed), 46, 47
Language, influence of, 22
Law, Department of (proposed), 112, 114, 117
Legislative-administrative relations, 14, 57, 68; role of criticism, 233 f.
Legislative investigating committees, 89, 149, 185
Legislature, *see* Congress
Library of Congress, 187, 195, 198, 201, 218
Licenses, orders governing, 157
Light House Service, 83
Limited jurisdiction, departments of: application of holding-company idea, 81, 86 ff.
Lincoln, Abraham, 159
Literature on, and studies of, administration, 8, 10-17, 39*n*, 44, 53*n*, 54*n*, 154, 176, 225, 233, 235
Local governments, *see* Governments
Long, Huey, 165

Machinery, utilization of, 107, 113, 119
Macmahon, A. W., 53*n*, 54*n*
Management, attitudes produced by purpose departments, 108, 109; by process departments, 119 ff.; capacities needed, 121 f., 127; assignment of specialist to leadership, 121
Managerial functions, control over, 187-93; allocation to independent

status, 196, 198; grouped in executive department, 199; allocation to Treasury, 202; individual consideration and allocation, 213; informal controls, 221
Mansfield, Harvey, 233
Marine Corps, 107
Maritime Commission, 49, 56, 82, 83, 84
Matériel, *see* Clientele
Mathematics, science of, 235
Mayors, assistant, 88
Means *v.* ends, 118, 123
Medical work, 106, 107, 112, 113, 115
Merit system, *see* Civil service
Military organization and administration, 4, 74 f.; security as factor in evolution of political forms, 22; necessity for unity of action, 75, 99, 116; proposed Dept. of National Defense, 81, 82, 87, 92, 100, 105, 116; maintenance upon regional basis, 138; *see also* War, Dept. of
Millett, J. D., 53*n*, 54*n*
Ministers of coördination, France, 44, 87
Multifunctional agencies developed on the basis of clientele or matériel, 123-31
Municipalities, relation to state government, 26; coördination of activities, 26; commission form of government, 30, 31; city-manager form, 34; grouping of departments under assistant mayors, 88; territorial departmentalization, 131; federal leadership, 142
Municipal Research, Bureau of, 11; studies by, publications, 11-17; sources, 13
Mussolini, Benito, 42, 44*n*

Namier, L. B., 8
National Archives, 187, 195, 198, 218
National Defense, Department of